One Life,

One List

The Ultimate Organisation System

To Create A Freedom Lifestyle

BRAND FOR SPEAKERS

Title: One Life, One List
Subtitle: The Ultimate Organisation System To Create A Freedom Lifestyle
Copyright © 2019

www.thechristianmoser.com
Follow me on LinkedIn: Christian Moser
(https://www.linkedin.com/in/thechristianmoser)
Follow me on Facebook: Christian Moser
(https://www.facebook.com/thechristianmoser)
Follow me on Instagram: @thechristianmoser
(https://www.instagram.com/thechristianmoser)

ISBN: 9781696261487

Book Design & Book Writing Coaching & Publishing Setup Done By:
Lily Patrascu
Brand for Speakers
www.brandforspeakers.com
+447557351222

Table Of Contents

Praise For The Book

"As a former world class athlete and Commonwealth Games Gold medallist, being organised is a key to success. Christian's book will help you to reach your greatest potential in business and life."

Steve Frew, the First Gymnastics Gold Medallist For Scotland in the History of the Commonwealth Games, www.SteveFrew.co.uk

"This easy-to-use detox program will help you tackle every inch of your life. That's what Christian Moser wants to teach in his book **One Life, One List.** *It's amazing and very practical. I was so astonished by his organising system in this book. It's like a life map to create a more productive freedom lifestyle.*

An organised life enables you to have more freedom, better health, and get more done. Christian helps you break down tasks and build routines over time so that life becomes simple, not overwhelming. I learnt how to master time management as time lost is never found. I learnt how to permanently organise closets and drawers, how to declutter rooms, how to organise travel plans, family vacations, shopping. This essential book will help you get the whole household organised and maintain the house decluttered.

I have read this very useful book and have started ruthlessly organising my home to unlock and re-invest wasted time. Love the concept of organising one room at a time as it keeps me focused, as otherwise it could be overwhelming to organise everything at the same time.

If you have considered buying this book DO IT - you will NOT regret it....

I highly recommend this book to anyone. It's a must have in your library!"

Teuta Avdyli - Author Of The Book "Born To Stand Out, Not To Fit In", Empowerment, Spiritual & Positive Parenting Coach

"This book couldn't have entered into my life at a more suitable time. I'm in the process of moving home, and I am a person that likes to keep things that aren't needed "just in case". Christian's **One Life, One List** *method has shown me how I can still be prepared without the additional clutter. His system will transform your life! Use it!"*

Hermione B Sihukai — Founder Of "The Sihukai Method", High-Performance Healing Coach, Co-Founder Of The Awakened Women Business Collective Ltd And International Speaker

"After reading Christian's book, not only did it take me on his journey but also on mine, as parallel realms. I can relate so much - especially one of his paragraphs - "Have you ever been able to create something unbelievable out of the worst darkness and pain?"

Christian has highlighted once again that it does not matter what you have been through, it does not matter what your situation looks like, if you want it, the universe will bring in the experiences you most desire. Living is a beautiful thing. Thank you Christian."

Sandro Heitor - Property Entrepreneur, Wealth Creator With A Difference, Author Of The Book "The Entrepreneur Paradox"

*"The ultimate to decluttering your life. I never considered myself a hoarder, but after living in our old house for several years I acquired some "stuff". After a couple of months in my new house I still couldn't find most things. If you are serious about changing your old habits and improving your current situation, then **One Life, One List** is a must read. This book changed my life, it will definitely change yours."*

Dee Lana - Motivational speaker, Award Winning Author Of The Book "Get Stuff Done", Founder Of Sweet Women Business Group, Successful Mentor, Independent Travel Agent

"The Book **One Life, One List** is a must read for all entrepreneurs who want to build a sustainable business system from anywhere in the world."

Jimmy Asuni, Author Of The Book "Dare To Be Imperfect", Motivational Speaker & Banker

Foreword By Harry Sardinas
Public Speaking, Empowerment
and Leadership Coach

I met Christian Moser at a personal development course. The minute I saw him, I knew there was something special about him, I just could not pinpoint what that was. He was highly energetic and always had a beautiful smile. I could sense he was very powerful as a coach and we had another thing in common – a need for freedom and fun.

As an empowerment, public speaking and leadership trainer, I help thousands of people every year to find the powers within in the face of adversity, overcome the fear of speaking and become confident speakers with my Speakers Are Leaders programme – www.SpeakersAreLeaders.com.

I believe the Universe has brought Christian to me not by chance, but because he is one of the people I see a huge potential for. I regularly meet tens of thousands of people a year at my empowerment and speaking workshops, and I see the potential in each one of them.

But for Christian I see that after attending the Entrepreneurs Are Leaders event, and the Speakers Are Leaders training at the Millionaire Speakers Network I organise, he has the potential to touch the lives of 100 million people with his ultimate organisation system, One Life, One List.

This is all possible because he had a wonderful great idea, he put it into practice, he turned it into a world-changing concept in this book and he pulled up the courage to speak on stage at my events. After thirty-five years of waiting to make his dream come true, he is now ready to share the stage with inspirational people, multimillionaires and celebrities at my upcoming events.

Just at the Entrepreneurs Are Leaders event I organised, he pulled up the courage to speak on the same stage where celebrities had spoken just a few hours before – celebrities like Marie Diamond, feng shui expert from the movie, *The Secret*; Eric Ho, "The Millionaire Monk" with 500k+ subscribers on YouTube; Armand Morin, the multimillionaire marketing expert, and royal advisor Chris Imafidon.

I am proud of what he has achieved so far and my heart is full of joy to see how coachable he is and what a great implementer he is, thanks to his organisation style. I have never met anyone as organised and as easy to work with as Christian. I wish him all the best and I am looking forward to implementing his revolutionising strategies that will impact the world.

I am grateful that his journey to become who he was meant to be started at Speakers Are Leaders. I highly recommend you buy his book and hope to see you soon at one of his One Life, One List workshops.

Harry Sardinas
Author of *Speakers Are Leaders*
www.SpeakersAreLeaders.com
www.EntrepreneursAreLeaders.com
www.MillionaireSpeakersNetwork.com
www.TopCoach.Org.UK

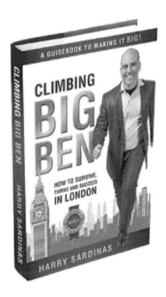 

About The Book

One Life, One List is the ultimate organisation tool to help you gain financial, personal, choice and time freedom. Its simplicity makes it affordable for anyone who wants more out of life. This book is based on the world-changing transformational One Life, One List system and upcoming app to help you manage your life and your business effectively and efficiently.

My Story

Imagine a little house in the middle of nowhere in the Black Forest, in the South of Germany, and a young, innocent and lively frail boy with not a care in the world. That boy was me. My life was smooth and very comfortable. Luckily, I have great parents. Thank God, they are alive and healthy at the age of eighty.

Growing up, I was highly disciplined but slightly introverted. Had you been there with me, you would have seen me explore the hills and the forest on a daily basis in my thick waterproof boots with my light backpack. The fresh air in the hills smelled like home. Had you accompanied me on my daily expeditions to the forest, you would have found great tranquility and calm in the trees and the stillness of the forest.

I knew everything there was to know within a radius of not more than ten miles around this little house. I never thought about the finiteness of life and it appeared endless, without troubles. There was nothing that could have warned me about what was to come.

I enrolled in the compulsory military. If you had watched over my bed, you would have seen how much discipline the army instilled in me. The military taught me the concept of needing to be always ready for everything. I learnt you've got to be ready for an attack or a natural disaster by being organised and knowing exactly where everything is.

Luckily, my mum was a multi-project manager. She is such an inspiration to me because she had a recipe for everything. She had a process or a system made up of several lists for literally anything she needed done. She was doing most things around the house and she knew that if she was gone on a trip or something, my father and I would perhaps not be able to get certain things done without having the step-by-step instructions written down, even for simple things like boiling an egg.

So she had Post-it notes pasted everywhere around the house, including how to cook certain meals we always had. From the most basic to the most complex tasks – she had it all written and pasted next to the place where the task had to be done. I didn't realise at the time how lucky I was to have such an organised mum.

My mum's organisation strategies served me in the army where you really do have to be organised or risk huge penalties, or even your life. I became passionate about IT the minute I bought my first computer. A friend of mine and I created a small IT company where we created software products which are partly still running today, worldwide.

In the middle of the Nineties I created one of the first quality insurance software systems, based on this new operating system called Windows. We sold the software worldwide and it felt like I was on top of the world.

One of the happiest moments of my life was the day I got married. Months later, my wife was pregnant and I was overjoyed at the thought of being so close to my dream of having a complete family, with kids. I was looking forward to a comfortable life in this small Black Forest town where we lived.

Have you ever expected a marvellous thing to happen and had your dreams crushed in front of your eyes? Nothing could have prepared me for what was to come. Ten days before the estimated date of birth, a problem occurred and an emergency caesarean section had to be performed. Seven days of anxiety and worry followed. Our child was in the incubator but her organs did not start functioning.

In the end, we had to switch off the machines. Melanie died and my whole world turned black. The loss of one of the most precious beings on Earth cut through deeper than I ever thought possible. I didn't think I could live with the pain, but somehow I survived.

Have you ever been able to create something unbelievable out of the worst darkness and pain? The Universe works in mysterious ways. A few weeks after my daughter died, I felt the need to get rid of material things because nothing seemed to matter to me anymore, and to make space for new creative energies to take their place.

I am a very creative person so every day I would pile up my endless ideas, but unfortunately very little got done because I didn't have a structure or a sequence to do it. I was unsure where I was going to start. I had a house jammed full of stuff from bottom to the top. I was collecting paperwork, data, business cards and so much clutter.

I had this big dream of having a freedom lifestyle, yet it was nowhere to be seen. I realised all the systems, technologies and methods learnt from others were not helpful for me because none of them had a logical tree structure. I remember one day when I made my decision to declutter and get rid of anything that wasn't absolutely necessary.

As I was letting things go to charity, I was letting depression, a feeling of failure, go as well. I was trying to create something new. That moment, twenty years ago, was the crystallisation of the One Life, One List system. Have you ever felt like everything in life happens for a reason? I have my mum to thank for being the inspiration for the One Life, One List system.

Without her carefully written notes, templates and procedures posted around the house, maybe the One Life, One List system would never have been created. Thanks to her, millions of people around the world can have a happier, easier, more productive life. I didn't know that at the time, of course. I was just using the system I created to live my life with joy and ease.

My second child was born and I became so grateful for being blessed with such an amazing child. After his birth, I took a lot of time to self-reflect and concluded I wanted to pursue a relationship with a man. I felt the need to reinvent myself and start my life from scratch, as if nothing had happened.

I wanted to erase from my mind the things that hadn't worked; the death of my precious child I was so looking forward to looking after, the feelings of helplessness that were chasing me around, the imminent divorce I knew was looming. I went into a deep depression and needed psychiatric help, therapy and horrible medication.

Finally, I managed to get rid of the feeling of helplessness and depression and had a complete recovery. I moved to Cologne, where I got a freelance contract as an IT consultant in a big German company. I got married to a man and things seemed rosy again. I was as happy as anyone could be ... until the day my life changed forever.

I was driving on a sunny day to the south of Germany to visit my family. My doctor called me up with a shiver in his voice and I sensed something really bad was going to happen, I just could not put my finger on it. My doctor had discovered during a routine checkup that I was infected with HIV.

One more terrible piece of news and yet this time I was willing to fight for my life. I had a strong feeling I was going to be okay.

Luckily medication has advanced a lot and I had the opportunity to find the best expert in the world, who became my doctor. Professor Dr Rockstroh is an international expert in HIV and hepatitis-C infection and, thanks to him, I am still alive today.

After a few years of on and off treatment, I got a type of cancer due to the HIV infection, so had to undergo surgery and chemotherapy. Since then I have been much more aware of my health; therefore, I do a routine checkup every three months where I can adjust my health parameters. And the most important thing is that now I am aware of it and I don't unwillingly infect others, which helps me reduce the spread of the virus.

Have you ever been in a situation where you think you can't possibly get worse than how you are doing now, and then you hit rock bottom? I got divorced again, driven by all the things that happened. Bang! I didn't have a penny to my name; my health was impacted and I was in a hopeless state.

The clock was ticking − I was already forty years old. That was the moment I realised I was always taking care of others, but never looking after my own physical, mental and emotional needs. I decided to fly solo, and take time to reflect. I flew to Bali. I had never been on a solo adventure before. I didn't even know that Bali was in Indonesia.

I booked a wonderful place in a beautiful villa operated by a wonderful couple. They are my best friends today. Klaus, an experienced man in his late sixties, shared a piece of advice which has ruled his whole life: "Follow your feelings." One day he told me about a transformational course recommended by his friends, who became extremely successful after doing it.

He put me in touch with them and this was the initial point of transformation of my life. I went to London and started to participate in the seminars and programmes of a worldwide organisation called Landmark. It was the first time in my life that I really got in touch with the real meaning of **transformation**.

Through Landmark, I got trained in the Team Leadership And Management programme and I transformed my communication by learning to honour integrity, commitment, promises and becoming powerful in making requests from others. I loved these new concepts that are a significant part of my code of honour now.

It really felt like I was back on track and I had the wisdom to know everything. That's what I thought. That's when I met transformational coach Dan Warburton and later the empowerment, leadership and public speaking trainer, Harry Sardinas, both awesome and cool guys with a unique outlook on life, just like me.

After all these years of enormous pain and struggles, it finally felt like I was on top of the world again. But there was one thing missing. My brain was full of awesome ideas, I was inspired about making a huge difference to the world, but I didn't really take the action which was needed to bring my ideas into existence. I started feeling lost, smoking weed and taking drugs as a way to escape my situation.

I was living in a world of illusions created by the consumption of the drugs. Under the influence of drugs, my reality was that everything was nice and everything worked as I was dreaming about. Whenever I came out of the influence of drugs, I would always say: "Christian, you know what to do. Your new life begins tomorrow." But tomorrow never came.

I started taking some action, but I was not focused and I had no plan whatsoever. Whenever something appeared difficult, I escaped into the world of drugs again. I loved daydreaming about how I was one day going to impact millions of people, but at the back of my mind I really doubted I had what it takes to get such a huge task done.

It was the New Year Celebration 2019 in Bali. I was rejoicing the special moment with friends for dinner and conversed about business. Triggered by a few wise words from my very good friend and business partner, Zul, from Surabaya, I woke up in the middle of the night and I made the decision to shift my whole life to another level.

I called my COO and we decided to shut down the office so that we would look for a new place and create something new. I was struggling with finance, staff and getting customers. We worked in a little space for a few months until we moved to our new office in the centre of Cologne. It is fifty metres from the wonderful historical cathedral and across from the main railway station.

Now I was ready for making it big in business. I had the cool office, the team, I was back in power and in control of my physical, mental and emotional needs. That's what I thought, but I was wrong. I realised that creating a powerful team and making teamwork a catapulting force for the growth of my company works only if there is a strong leadership, where people are inspired, motivated, are not complaining and are ready to stick together in times of hardship in order to achieve success.

I was searching for a better way to get my team touched, moved and inspired so that together we could grow as a company. That was the moment when I became aware of the Entrepreneurs are Leaders event in London, organised by "The Ultimate Entertainer", my friend Harry Sardinas, with whom I spent a great time in the Team Management And Leadership programme, and the personal branding and sales coach, Lily Patrascu.

This event was the most impactful event I've ever had in my life. It opened my eyes to a world I hadn't a clue about.

One Moment Can Change Your Life

I thought I was a great entrepreneur already. That's because in my business I'm surrounded by untransformed people, not ready to look outside the business and not willing to do things to go the extra mile.

It didn't make sense at the time but I knew deep inside it was the right move for me to book coaching with Dan, so I never hold back on any actions that must be taken and I can achieve my personal goals and inspire millions of people.

I took the coaching of Harry Sardinas so I could become unstoppable in my public speaking online and from huge conferences worldwide with thousands of people, and I started getting coached to enhance my personal brand and increase and monetise my influence with Lily Patrascu.

Lily Patrascu coached me on how to write my first book and how to turn the concept of One Life, One List into multiple ways of making a difference to the world, through the upcoming One Life, One List app, the online courses based on the One Life, One List philosophy of life, the entrepreneur networking groups centred on the luxury minimalism lifestyle and the daily videos in various social media streams, and many more ways of spreading the word through public speaking and keynote speaking.

For the very first time I was astonished at the impact my book could immediately have on millions of people. Here I was, having spent twenty years wandering around, and then getting my book published in two months after deciding to do it and, not only that, having the One Life, One List system – something that would impact people other than myself.

The ideas I'd had for over twenty years finally crystallised into this book you are currently holding in your hand. When you finally write your book, it feels like you are giving birth to a brand new baby. Can you imagine? If this book hadn't come to life, the One Life, One List philosophy of life could have died with me.

Now I'm keen on sharing my message through public speaking and I'm ready to make a difference in the world with my experience. I systemised my business with the One Life, One List system so I could fulfill my dream of working remotely worldwide. One of my charity projects, which involves helping my awesome friends in Ghana create a business by providing microfinancing and business coaching, is ramping up already, just a few days after the Entrepreneurs Are Leaders event.

First of all, at the event, I met a guy who was living in exactly the same little town where my Ghanaian projects are – in Tema, near Accra. Bingo! The power of networking and being in the right place at the right time. Simply because I pulled up the courage to speak on stage for a few minutes at Entrepreneurs Are Leaders, I met a Ghanaian who was inspired, gave me advice and shared his professional network of lawyers and other connections I needed.

In a few weeks, we are opening our first Blackmind pub in Ghana city so that we can create money to invest in the next step of the business there. I am inspired about supporting the Ghanaian Blackmind project in order to bring awareness of the African situation and its products to the world. The modules offered at Harry and Lily's events became essential in terms of giving me the structure I needed to realise my vision.

We are opening our new co-working space, Dom5.space, in the centre of Cologne and we are cooperating with other co-working spaces in Bali, Indonesia, and in Florida, USA, in terms of contributing to the worldwide community and the network.

The point of telling you my story is to inspire you to keep going despite any obstacles you may experience. The Universe is conspiring to help you become who you were meant to be. If I hadn't gone through all those painful experiences, maybe I would never have created the One Life, One List philosophy.

If I hadn't experienced excruciating pain, I would perhaps not understand the pain others feel on a daily basis as refugees. If I hadn't experienced leadership issues, I would perhaps not have gone to the Entrepreneurs Are Leaders event, which was the event that gave me the opportunity to find my own potential and share my message with millions of people.

If I hadn't struggled in my marriage, I would perhaps never have learnt to be as compassionate, organised, helpful and understanding as I am now. Your pain and your failure is the source of your biggest learning. I struggled all my life to fulfill my promises and follow up on the requests I made of others.

I created One Life, One List as a framework to make your life easy so you can be supported to apply all the strategies you learned in your life to improve your self-management.

The One Life, One List system is simple and accessible by anybody in the world. I am passionate about helping those in need and I know this system is going to help millions of people – including you, perhaps; that is, if you apply it!

I hope you will share your results from having applied the One Life, One List system and hope to meet you someday. There is nothing that will make me happier than putting a smile on your face because you have managed to double your productivity, reduce headaches and hassles, and instead spend more time creating that freedom lifestyle – whatever that means to you!

Note To The Reader

Dear Reader,

Maybe you are a creative entrepreneur, coming up with brilliant ideas every single day. If you are anything like me, you are excited every single day at the thought of one more thing you came up with today.

Maybe you are a business owner, or perhaps thinking about starting your online business. Perhaps you are obsessed with your vision of success, yet you simply don't know where to start, or where to go from here.

Maybe you are an entrepreneur dreaming of systemising and automating your business so you can keep more revenue and streamline processes. Maybe you want to save more time and raise your productivity.

Maybe you want to create more engagement with your customers or you want a particular app or software created for your company's goals. Maybe you want a particular IT project managed. Perhaps you are overwhelmed by all the daily tasks you need to do, or you simply don't know how to master technology so your business would grow exponentially.

Regardless of whether you are overwhelmed, you are looking for a more efficient way of systemising your business or you simply want to take your online business to the next level, I can help you.

The biggest thing I learnt, thanks to starting my career in quality management in the automotive industry, was that as a business owner, your focus has to be on making things easy.

Later on, whilst working as a developer, IT architect and IT project manager for some of the most powerful companies in the world, like Bosch, AXA and Siemens, I learnt that your focus has to be on streamlining your workflow, and creating procedures, templates and checklists, so that everyone knows exactly what to do and not a single step is missed.

I also learned that a business needs a stable and reliable infrastructure and a strategy to bring your extraordinary ideas into the world. You also need to create a sustainable income-producing business and that's what the most creative people sometimes forget.

I can teach you how to manage the IT side of your online business, how to automate and systemise your business based on One Life, One List system, how to upload files, how to manage your cloud and finally, how to collect all the information you need to present your products to the world so that people are inspired in an extraordinary way.

In a world where security breaches are costing companies millions in lost revenue, I can coach you in how to create a powerfully secure online business so you can prevent hacking, reduce e-commerce shopping issues and make your website(s) user friendly.

I'm looking forward to a successful partnership with you on your way to the success of your extraordinary ideas and products.

Innovation Separates Leaders From Followers

Acknowledgements

Thank you to Lily Patrascu with her Brand For Speakers programme for helping me turn my One Life, One List idea into a multitude of products and for helping me put into existence my idea which will impact the world in an extraordinary way. Lily helps you create extraordinary ideas that transform the world, and enhances your personal brand, so you can have more impact and influence worldwide, and so you can monetise your influence and make a difference.

Thank you to Lily Patrascu also for making me realise the extent of the impact my book could have through online courses, the community created around the One Life, One List system, keynote speaking and business coaching.

Lily helped me get my book created from start to finish, she helped me have the book published and exceptionally designed. Without her, this book would not have been possible. She gave me lots of ideas on how to create the user-friendly systems included in this book, so I could condense my expertise into blueprints anyone can follow, and also on how to monetise my knowledge through speaking. If you are looking to write your own book, you can contact Lily at hello@lily.global.

Chapter 1
The One Life, One List Philosophy

Why is everyone trying to make business appear to be so hard? The reality is that it doesn't have to be difficult – your business can be simplified with the One Life, One List way of life.

The One Life, One List philosophy is based on the principle that everything in your life can be organised based on a simple list. This is a system I have developed because I realised the power of freedom I managed to create in my life thanks to automating, organising, simplifying, systemising and decluttering my life and my business.

This gave me the sense of being able to have the freedom of choice to be anywhere, anytime, with anyone, and easily find the information I needed, without hassle. This also gave me the freedom to access any piece of information, document or item I needed, when I needed it, without hours of searching and time-wasting.

It also enabled me to create a lifestyle business where I suddenly started to feel in control of everything that was out of order in my life before. Thanks to this system I am able to travel anywhere, anytime, at a moment's notice, and keep my word with ease, keep my integrity intact, be always punctual, be seen as a man of his word, and keep my appointments and my promises.

The best part is that, regardless of circumstances, this system gives me the opportunity to be always ready for anything that could potentially occur during my travels. It gives me the latest cutting-edge list of luxury items that make my life easier, simpler, more carefree.

Knowing this system has freed up thousands of hours in my life and my business, and has given me the greatest gift of them all – TIME.

We chase money, we chase items to make us feel good, we chase everything until we finally realise, as we grow older, that we are running out of time, and being able to create extra minutes with our loved ones, with our friends, is absolutely priceless, because a business or job is meant to give you the opportunity to live the lifestyle that you really want.

I really believe this system can transform millions of people's lives, including yours; that is, if you apply it. There is a big difference between knowing something and taking the time to gradually implement it in your life.

This system can revolutionise and create a tremendous impact not only on your life, but on your business, on the way you do business, the promises you now get to keep with your family, friends, work colleagues or new relationships.

Double Your Productivity And Save Thousands Of Hours

It is really incredible what you can achieve once you liberate yourself from all those things that keep you from creating more wealth or saving money, that make you angry or frustrated daily – such as missing a piece of paper, being unable to find a receipt, your critical insurance cover at the moment you really need it, or your emergency contact details when you desperately need those, also.

This philosophy is centred on creating luxury minimalism in your life and getting rid of unnecessary items, which frees you up of clutter – space occupied in your mind and in your physical environment. When you get space, you are then free to be more creative, to have more joy, to have more freedom, to be more relaxed, to understand more closely what it is that you REALLY want to do with your life. When you have space and time you have THE ULTIMATE FREEDOM where you can create your future, the dream life you have been wanting for all your life.

The best part is that this philosophy is designed to enable you to achieve more with less, to help you get into helpful routines that create positive habits and to remind you to stay in touch with the people you meet, to expand your network and to be so organised that anyone could wake you up in the middle of the night and you would be able to know exactly where everything is, and you would be ready to leave at a moment's notice to take advantage of any speaking, travel, business or leisure opportunity.

I understand this way of life may not suit everybody. You may just like to use this blueprint as a way of systemising your business, your groceries, your family life. You may choose to use this philosophy as a way to organise any aspect of your life.

The cool part is that you can customise this system to your particular situation, whether you need to organise a conference, a product launch, a marketing campaign, your entire business, your children's parties or even your own recipes. It is an all-encompassing solution for anyone who wants to be organised.

If you are an expat, you will find this philosophy will give you peace of mind as you are travelling and will keep everything you could possibly need within easy reach so you are always prepared for your next venture, your next business deal or your next trip around the Himalayas.

At a time when information is everywhere, many entrepreneurs are overwhelmed. This way of life is an ultra-simple, efficient and effective way of living your life so you can do more of what you love and less of what you hate.

The One Life, One List Philosophy is based on several guiding principles for each part of your life that needs organising.

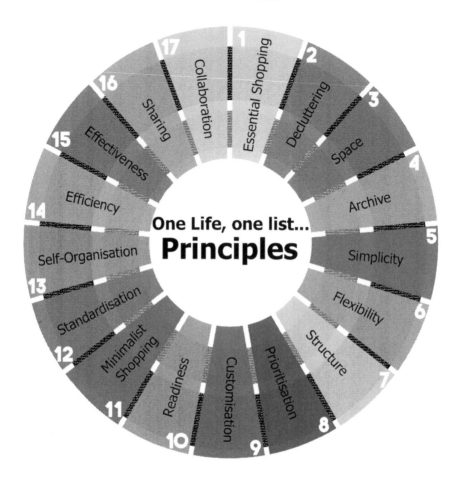

The principles at the core of One Life, One List lifestyle philosophy are:

1. **Essential Shopping**
2. **Decluttering**
3. **Space**
4. **Archive**
5. **Simplicity**
6. **Flexibility**

7. **Structure**

8. **Prioritisation**

9. **Customisation**

10. **Readiness**

11. **Minimalist Shopping**

12. **Standardisation**

13. **Self-Organisation**

14. **Efficiency**

15. **Effectiveness**

16. **Sharing**

17. **Collaboration**

This philosophy of life is crystallised into the **One Life, One List System** I am currently developing into an app and a planner to support and accompany the simplification of your life. This system has multiple subsystems that guide my life and my business and I am certain they can make a considerable difference to your life, too.

These are the systems at the core of One Life, One List System:

1. **Luxury Minimalism System**

2. **Wardrobe System**

3. **Hotel System**

4. **Backpack System**

5. **Network System**

6. **Travel System**

7. **Emergency System**

8. **Security System**

9. **Office System**

10. **Stack System**

11. **Notation System**

12. **Income Tracker System**

13. **Excellent Habits System**

14. **Accountability System**

15. **Self-Reflection System**

16. **Well-being System**

17. **Wisdom System**

18. **Relationship Management System**

19. **Balance System**

20. **The Community System**

Chapter 2
Start With Decluttering

If you are one of those entrepreneurs, consultants, speakers, mums or ordinary people who are almost buried in paperwork or general house clutter – I know exactly how that feels. For many years that was me.

Until I realised I really needed to do something to get rid of anything that was holding me back because I wanted to find a way to always keep my promises and I could not figure out how to do it when I could not find what I needed at the right time.

That is precisely why the One Life, One List system starts with a big decluttering of your life and business. However, before that you need to buy some key items that will help you stay organised.

Buy The Essentials You Need For Decluttering

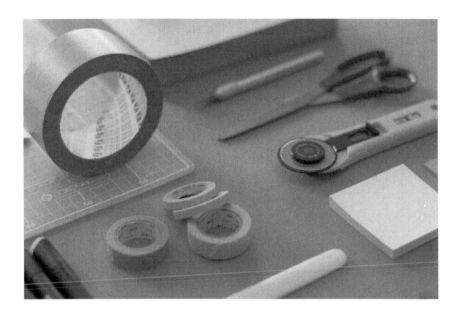

Here is what you will need for decluttering, both initially and on an ongoing basis, in order to maintain a sense of freedom and space:

- scissors – for cutting off any labels with your address on them, to protect your identity;
- a powerful paper-shredder – I recommend the Leitz brand as it tends to be a great one;
- strong plastic boxes for getting rid of expired items, old things that need to go directly to the rubbish;
- recycling boxes or recycling bags by type – for paper, glass, tins, or clothing for the charity shop, plus various

other items for giveaway websites like gumtree.com or freecycle.org;

- a great labeller – where you can type and have the label printed off – you can find some great inexpensive ones on amazon.com;

- container boxes that fit your existing space exactly on your shelf, cupboard, wardrobe;

- five boxes for mail, tagged with these labels: Incoming Mail, Recycle, To File, Urgent, Receipts;

- file separators – so you can place your files in relevant file holders; and,

- clear plastic file holders – for separating projects.

Space

=

Freedom

Create An Empty Space

This is one of the most revolutionising – yet so simple – methods I have created that has the biggest impact. When I declutter my apartment, I literally empty out all my apartment. I take everything out of the apartment and I put it into storage. As the apartment is now empty, I am able to create space and only bring back in those items I really – and I mean really – need. I am talking about absolute necessities.

I don't keep anything that doesn't bring me joy and I certainly don't keep anything that doesn't fit my body, my current state of mind, my personality, my current style, or my updated personal brand. I then start putting things exactly where they belong, because I now have a lot of space from decluttering the apartment.

Then I can add new things, or even assign a particular space for important things. After a day of decluttering, things that are no longer useful or important can be moved to a dump, a charity shop or offered as freebies to friends. There are websites where you are able to trade off things you no longer need, or allow other people to purchase them for a symbolic amount and collect them from your house.

Free your mind by following this process and take back into your home or your office only the things you need. The alternative is to remove absolutely everything from one room and to put it into another room so you are able to see everything clearly. Then you can clean the room up and give it a fresh look, perhaps by painting it, adding some flowers or whatever makes you happy, and only bring back in the items that give you joy.

It may take you a while to do this if you have a large house, so ask yourself: "How can I declutter my house faster?" Maybe you can enlist some friends to help you out. Maybe you can enrol the children into doing it with you, or perhaps even take a couple of days at the weekend to do it gradually. You will not believe the amazing results you can achieve by doing this.

Declutter

Take time and plan slowly to remove from your house the things you no longer need. Once you decide that certain items are no longer needed, dump them all at once. Make it a habit to do it weekly or at least twice a month. If you have a lot of spare time, you can decide if you want to sell some of the things that can be used again or just donate them to people who are in need.

If you are really busy, assign a particular room or even just a particular area of your room to be decluttered. If you really don't have much time, start with decluttering a drawer, a shelf, or even your office table. Just get started, then build momentum.

Create A Blank Slate

The reason why many entrepreneurs and many people in general fail to get organised and instead are continuously overwhelmed by tasks is because they never take the time to do what I would call a "deep clean" of the list of things they need to do – almost like an amnesty – where they forgive themselves for what they did and what they didn't do, and then start afresh.

How it works is, you copy everything – and I really mean everything – from your lists that are everywhere in your house and your office and wherever else, and then you rewrite them or move them all together onto a fresh list.
The act of clearing out all your lists from everywhere gives you that feeling as if you were a newborn baby who now has all sorts of options, whereas before you may have felt a bit constrained by having too many things to do.

You may have lists written on your fridge, in your notebook, on your PC, in different Excel spreadsheets and project software, in your bathroom, in your recipe book ... pull them all together and put them into a file called "Temporary Archive". That way, you move every single thing you had to do into a different place, where it is not bothering you anymore.

The benefit is that when you look at your fridge, your notebook, or any of the other places you kept your to-do lists, you get to see a clean space where you can create freely. When your space is cluttered, it is very easy to get overwhelmed and it is very hard to get creative and find solutions for problems.

The minute you declutter your to-do lists and start from zero, you have the opportunity to create new solutions and to see what is perhaps not required anymore on your to-do lists. I recommend you use an Excel spreadsheet or a paper-based daily planner for your "Temporary Archive" until the One Life, One List app is ready.

Allow only those to-do list items that you really want and need to do to migrate from your "Temporary Archive" to the active lists in your One Life, One List system. You will find a large number of things may not be needed anymore.

Archive

Archive everything that is no longer important, but keep those items in the archive for future reference, for as long as you would like to hold on to them.

The One Life, One List system is a way of life that is based on simplicity and flexibility.

Choose Simplicity

Simplicity And Flexibility

The basis of the entire system is that it can be done with something as simple as a pen and paper. That is why I LOVE this system. It grants access to millions of people, who are able to implement it without any hassle.

Decluttering your life starts with first, decluttering your mind, and second, decluttering your overall to-do list. From the moment you do both, you will gain a sense of freedom you have perhaps not experienced in a long time. The idea behind the system is that you create one single list where you can manage absolutely everything that's on your mind.

The first step is to write down literally every little thing that you want to do, be, achieve, experience, buy or whatever as an unstructured list. You simply brainstorm and write down every thought or action plan to create one big list. You can do this at whatever time of day suits you – perhaps initially as you wake up in the morning or just before going to bed, when you are the least stressed.

You then create a structure by clustering and arranging your list; group together all the actions or the items that are part of the same type. For example, if you need to buy tomatoes, potatoes, shoes and a notebook, you put all the items to be bought together on a shopping list.

You can also group together all the items that are related to your business or a particular project in your business.

Unify All Lists

Unify all the lists by grouping things together. You could create a checklist for your gym plan, one to track your money, a checklist for the movies you want to see, the books you want to read, the things you want to do in the morning, the new projects you want to tackle, the customers you have, and all the current projects that you're managing.

You can create multiple lists such as: reading lists, wish lists, travel destination lists, theatre shows you want to see, party checklists, etc.

Plan One List Then Create A Sublist

If you want to become organised, the first thing you need to do is to create a name tag for the list. After a while, if you want to organise your business, structure the key things you need to achieve for your customers in a list. Things in your brain tend to be structured in clusters, so if you organise everything in lists and sublists it will become easier to get more things done.

In the case of your shopping list, mentioned above, you can divide that into sublists, if you need to, so that you have a list for each type of shop you need to visit or each shopping trip you need to make.

The best part about organising yourself with lists and sublists is that you will be able to focus only on a particular sublist, meaning you get less overwhelmed by the numerous things you have to do in all the different areas of your life.

Prioritise

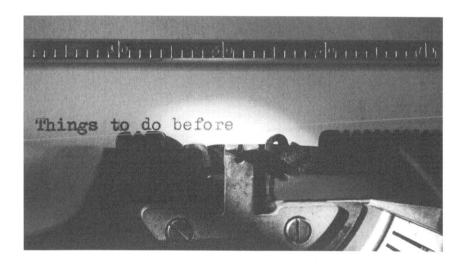

It's a good idea to prioritise the things on your list, so that you make sure you focus on those things that most need your attention. For example, you could label things as:

- A = urgent and important;
- B = important but not urgent;
- C = urgent but not important; and,
- D = not urgent, not important.

In the case of category D items, you might want to think again about whether you need to do them at all!

Rearrange The Tasks On Your Lists

Create your daily importance and daily urgency list from the brainstorm you did. The most important part now is to put every part of each list in the right sequence so that you are clear about which task goes first, second, third, etc. Once the One Life, One List app is created you will be able to do this easily, but in the meantime you can just number the tasks in order of priority, then begin doing the task at the very top of the list.

Customise Your List As You Like

Decorate your list as you like – whether that is by using different colours for different types of events, to-do lists, birthdays, or by using different types of notations, abbreviations or stickers to accompany those events. This will enable you to make certain things stand out in your list.

Structure the list as you wish. Remember that you are the master of your list. Choose to move stuff around as you please in a way that makes sense to you.

Do Not Be A Slave To Your List.

Let The List Be Your Slave.

Chapter 3
The Luxury Minimalism System

The luxury minimalism system is a core principle of the One Life, One List system in simplifying your life. It all starts with having the right mindset. Athletes have this "mind over body" motivation in order to conquer fatigue and fear. It is not limited to the body, it is more like "Mind over EVERYTHING".

I don't want time to dictate my daily stuff. I want to be the one dictating what is going to happen next. For that reason, I have discovered the ultimate way of managing my time. The ultimate way of creating time freedom is based on the law of accumulation.

Measure The Time You Spend On Different Activities

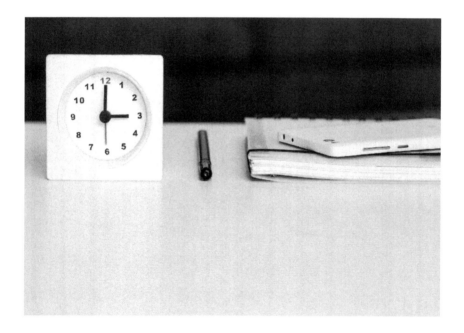

Track the time you spend daily. You will realise so much time goes to waste and is not helping you further your goals. Why is it that billionaires have the same twenty-four hours in a day and are able to get so much more done? It is because they have found efficient and effective ways of working.

Add up all the hours you spend doing different activities. You will find you are spending an awful lot of time choosing your clothes, queueing in supermarkets, or on the bus, in the car or on the way to different places.

If you are a regular business traveller, you will find that you spend a lot of time packing your bags, waiting for your suitcases at the airport after having checked them in, buying again things that break regularly, looking for receipts for your tax returns, looking for items you have misplaced or mislabelled on your computer or in your house.

This lack of planning and organisation could have a terrible impact not only on you but also on the wealth you are able to create, and the relationships you have with your business partners, spouse or children. It could lead to endless arguments, blaming each other, anger and frustration.

The common recurring theme is time wasted, whereas it should be time invested in your future dream life. The best way to be in control of how much time you spend on a certain task or the energy you spend on that task is to do every task in the smallest possible amount of time.

The question you should ask yourself is, "How can I reduce waste in my life? How can I calculate what takes the most time in my life? How can I ensure each task takes the least amount of time, yet has an extraordinary result?"

If you take 30 minutes a day to choose your outfit, then you will have wasted 10,950 minutes a year or 109,500 minutes in ten years of your life. That is 1,825 hours you could have used for something you love to do.

I focus 100% of my time on reducing every aspect of my life that is a waste of time so that I have more time for my child, more time to enjoy and be contented with what I am doing, more time for travelling and more time for having fun and keeping fit.

Keep Only Necessary Items

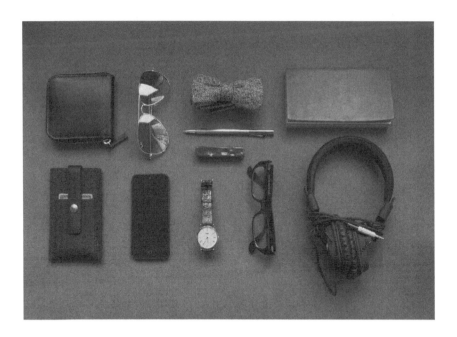

The most important part of luxury minimalism is to keep what you need, buy what you need and throw away what you don't need. You may buy new things because you believe these things will help you in your daily living or may help you do your work faster and easier.

But, once you have purchased something new, have regular routine scheduled checks in your wardrobe, house and office to eliminate what no longer serves you. If you are like me, maybe you sometimes become sentimental about things you purchased because they are the product of your hard work.

These items may be broken and not able to be fixed and yet you still keep them. They may be clothes that no longer fit you or look great on you. They may be empty boxes or jars. They may be expired food, make-up, perfume, toiletries. They may be ripped or torn clothes, old-fashioned jewellery, old computers, old software, CDs you know you will never listen to, art books you will never look at, old bedding or even plastic bags.

If you love hoarding things, this exercise will be the hardest and yet the most liberating one of them all. You must find the courage, the time and the power to let old things go, to throw away unwanted, unnecessary things so you can create the space in your life to move forward.

Keep Things Really Neat

Make an effort to be organised from the moment you wake up. Start your morning routine with keeping your bed tidy and neat, as that will give you a feeling of satisfaction and motivation to keep going.

Keep Things In Labelled Containers

To avoid important things being thrown or given away, you need to put items in some sort of labelled stackable folder, jar, box or container. Its purpose is to allow you to easily locate the item and minimise the space you use in your home or office. Square-shaped containers are better than round ones as they optimise space usage.

Design Your Own Luxury Lifestyle

Luxury minimalism doesn't mean living like a monk or doing yoga all day. Just get rid of all the things that hold you back from getting what you want. Get rid of the clutter that is not allowing you to live a contented, free lifestyle. Get rid of the items that trip you up on the way to the kitchen or the office, the items that block your energy, the things that make you or keep you unhappy in your house.

Find an easier way to store things so you can easily reach them each time. If you want to lose weight but the sports kit is hard to reach, consider changing its location so you can have what you use most frequently within easy reach.

If you are a frequent flyer, find a way to place suitcases in a great spot in your house without having them fall on top of your head every time you need to get them out.

No False Economy

I am very careful not to hold on to items that may actually make me lose money because they are cheap. Many people invest in cheap things but I advise against it because expensive items with a great brand tend to be luxury, quality, look great, make you feel good, and make you feel like you are worth it, plus they tend to have a great exchange or return policy.

I savour every moment I get to spend listening to my Bose music box, the experience I get to have whilst shaving my beard with the top quality Philips shaver, the feeling of brushing my teeth with my Philips Sonicare toothbrush. If you feel you can't afford these items, I am here to tell you that **you can't afford not to** own classy items, because cheaper items will cost you more in the long run.

Cheaper items tend to break faster and could end up leaving you stranded at the exact moment you need that particular thing. Samsonite or Tumi suitcases are my favourite brands because they have a great design and they can last ten years, whilst cheaper ones may break every single time you travel and you may even be embarrassed, coming with your cheap-looking suitcases to the airport.

Invest In Whatever Luxury Means To You

Invest In Quality Shoes

Choose comfortable, great-looking, classy shoes that you can use for multiple purposes so that you are ready for most opportunities that come along and so that you are always looking great and feeling amazing.

People always check out your shoes so keep something in your arsenal that makes them look shiny and cared for at all times. It takes only a few seconds to create a first impression, so make it an excellent one.

Be Prepared.

It Is The

Only Way

To Succeed.

The "Be Always Ready" Principle

This principle has revolutionised many aspects of my life. I am a frequent traveller and I get many opportunities to coach my clients in their place of business and that is why it is so important to me to be able to travel to a new location without hassle and wasting time.

I learnt this in the army and it has been one of the most powerful and life-changing systems I have learnt. When you are in the army you need to "be always ready" to get up and go. You don't have time to pack your bags or take your time.

This is something that has proven so useful to me over the years, as most people waste so much time and so many opportunities because they are not organised. That is why preparation is very important. You do need to take the time to take care of the details that will become important last minute.

Do you have all the papers you need with you for your meetings? Are they tidy and organised? Are your shoes polished? Is your place tidy when you get back from work? This principle has saved me thousands of pounds and hours, time and money I could otherwise have wasted, and has brought me enormous comfort, happiness, and freedom to work anywhere.

The Minimalist Shopping Principle

The minimalist shopping principle is about taking control of your shopping so that shopping doesn't take control of you. Have you ever experienced a moment when you wake up in the morning, about to have an important meeting, only to find there is no cereal in the cupboard and no milk in the fridge?

You go to put on your socks, but they are torn, so you go looking for another pair but they are not paired up as they are all in the wash. You then go to brush your teeth and you just about manage to squeeze one drop of toothpaste because you were too busy to do the shopping.

You then go to the store, but there is a huge queue. For time-savvy entrepreneurs, shopping can be an easy, automated system where you never need to waste time and always have what you need handy.

Schedule Your Shopping

If you really want to save time and money, you need to schedule your shopping so you are clear on where and when you will buy those products. I like buying things on Saturdays as that is when I feel most relaxed, though the ideal time for shopping is actually on Tuesdays, when there is the least number of shoppers in the store.

The worst time to buy things is actually after work during the week, because that is when you are likely to waste the most time queueing. I find it even more frustrating to purchase items using the automated checkout machines as that takes even longer.

I have a checklist of where I personally buy everything, which includes my size, the names of the stores I purchase from/the brands I purchase, and the type of item, which means if I had a secretary or a virtual assistant, I could easily pass that person the list and they could do the ordering of that item for me online, which again could save me time.

Some brands have slight size differences so that is why it is a good idea to make a note of the specific brand size you need, for example. Buying things while they are on sale is also a great idea as you can then have more money to spend on what you love. I tend to be on newsletter mailing lists for most brands I love, so I am always kept updated with regard to the best quality items.

Invest In Quality Exclusive Items

I am a great believer in luxury items as they tend to be good quality products and they last longer than cheap ones. My clothing and my home are important to me. They say that what you wear and what your home looks like will define who you really are and what you do.

Personal comfort at home will dictate the level of stress you have and your ability to switch off from your work problems. Keep your house clean, organised, and consistent with your preferred colours that make you feel relaxed. I like to redefine my future by creating as much space as possible and by investing in durable products with a sleek cutting-edge look.

Experience Luxury Your Way

You may have something you consider a luxury. Define it – what is it for you in particular? For some people it could mean owning a painting and staring at it all day; for others it could be watching football, buying particular brands of suits, bags, jewellery or shoes, spending time travelling or staying in luxury hotels.

I buy my shoes in London. I love to do this because I can. That is my luxury. The experience makes me feel I am worth it. Whilst sipping a cup of organic juice or enjoying a perfectly designed meal created by a chef on the beach in

Bali, whilst also listening to a DJ playing soft beats, I feel the world is my oyster.

There are certain experiences that make you feel like you are in paradise. Write down these desired experiences on your wish list and start investing in what you consider a luxury.

When I want to relax I go to Bali to a villa and I travel in luxury because I work very hard. I have a good flight and I meet my friends in Jakarta in a bar. I can enjoy that because there is nothing in my apartment besides an old television, so I can travel anywhere without worrying about being burgled.

Buy The Best When You Need Something

You can't attract great clients or investors whilst you are embarrassed. It is best to have a smaller number of quality items and invest a larger amount of money in them than to have a greater quantity of things and look terrible. Investing in great quality items enables you to reduce the time you need to spend shopping for new items, which in turn helps you automate and systemise your life.

It also helps to save the environment, as we clearly do not need more items to be thrown in the oceans or to pollute the planet.

Replace Older Items With Smaller Cutting-Edge Ones

I tend to replace bigger older items with the smaller version of the same thing as I am always looking for lighter ways to travel around the world. For example, I always look out for the best quality containers or receptacles for my toiletries, toothbrush, shavers, socks, backpacks, wallets, because having everything handy and organised is very important to me.

Invest In Transformational Gadgets

I always try to get as much leverage as I possibly can from any item I invest in. I am always looking for that small, perfect item that can make a huge difference in my life. What you will find most of the time is that the smaller the item, the bigger the difference.

Invest in small gadgets that can transform your life. I love using quality things such as my Mercedes car, my GoPro camera, the tripod for my camera. I love techy things because that enables me to use powerful gadgets that make my life easier. They might be really expensive, but they are worth it.

Chapter 4
The Wardrobe System

This system involves getting my wardrobe organised so that I never struggle to find everything I need inside my wardrobe. I prefer a standardised minimalist wardrobe. Whilst this concept may not suit everyone, and perhaps especially not women, the idea of it can help you to have all the items needed for personal comfort within easy reach.

The preset checklist I mentioned earlier comes in really useful here.

Dress For Impact

Dress For Impact

For a man, in particular, it is important to invest in a few quality items that can be used frequently, such as a powerful gorgeous-looking watch, beautiful shoes, and a really great suit, shirt and quality cufflinks.

For men in particular, because of the lack of variety in outfits, it is important to spend more on these items so you really get something that gets that "wow" impression from people so you are kept in people's minds as someone memorable.

Whenever I go shopping, I stick to the same brands which means that I get notified of any special deals they have and I get to look great all the time. I get treated well because I look great, and I attract better clients and better opportunities as a result. Dress as you want to be addressed.

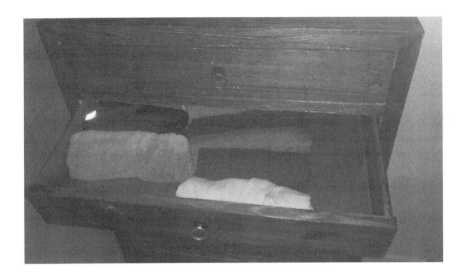

Before you buy something to wear consider the specific shops that sell all of your desired clothes so you save time. Men typically buy one hundred pairs of socks, but I normally buy two or three of them. I like to buy things that are easily colour-matched, such as black, grey and white.

That helps me blindly go to my wardrobe and choose something that matches without taking too much of my time.

Dress According To Your Brand

Your personal brand is important, whether you are aware of it or not. The way you are perceived makes the difference between being able to charge more for the same work or not. For every keynote speech I deliver, the event promoters expect me to dress in accordance with my brand colours.

They have certain implied expectations of me, such as wearing a very polished business suit that makes me look professional and presentable. That is why I use specific shops that sell branded trendy items.

As a minimalist, I pack very light when travelling, but everything I have represents my brand. Having stylish and high-quality clothes makes it very easy for me to represent my brand anywhere I go.

Chapter 5
The Hotel System

Have you ever experienced the situation where you go to a hotel and you feel so much better than at home? That is because there is no clutter around. Everything is perfectly organised and in a suitable place. This is exactly the same concept.

Organise your house like a hotel; give yourself space in every area of your life and that will give you the opportunity to finally create freedom. When I travel, I spend my life in an apartment or in a hotel. I prefer to stay in a hotel because I don't want to bother my friends or acquaintances.

If I travel for two weeks, I am in another hotel almost every day as I like to fully experience life. I always live out of the box – well, technically, out of the suitcase. Whilst being in a hotel, I noticed I was always in flow, always much more productive, taking so much more action when I was abroad.

So, I thought how about if I turned my own home into a hotel instead of an apartment, so I can maintain the same level of productivity? Whilst travelling, I realised I don't need more than a bed and some basic clothes to feel comfortable.

Since then I always organise my room as a hotel when I leave. I take the time to clean up after myself and to keep my entire house tidy, which means I could technically rent it out to others. I don't currently do it but I like having the option, as I don't like any sort of waste.

There are a lot of companies that rent out their flats so I know that if I rent out my flat I could potentially earn extra income that I could use for my leisure activities.

Chapter 6
The Backpack System

Imagine travelling with only a piece of hand luggage. That is the easiest way to travel for me. How is that possible? Simple; I only need two shirts when I travel. I love travelling with just one backpack. I have found the perfect backpack, which is packed according to my preset checklist.

Everything is placed in an organised way, in small folders and zipped plastic bags or plastic containers.

I have a checklist of the number of items I need to feel comfortable at any time. For example, I know how many pairs of socks, shirts, suits, and any item of clothing I need for a certain length of time. I have standard packing lists for three-day short trips or for a one week or two week holiday, so that whenever I need to leave I have everything ready.

It is very important that every single item has an assigned spot inside my backpack so if there were an earthquake or some sort of emergency I could pick up my backpack and be ready to go.

I usually have these items inside my backpack: my passport, a credit card, a wallet, energy powerbanks, universal power adaptors, all the items I need for my personal maintenance, such as a toothbrush, toiletries, shaver, emergency medicine. I usually keep a seven-day reserve of medicine with me and all required paperwork in a specific place, which is essential. Whatever happens, I am ready to go.

There should be a hidden safe place for your passport inside your bag. You need to get into the habit of putting it straight back when you take it out so that you know exactly where to find it at all times. I have a space in the left-hand-side of the backpack assigned for my business cards. I put all my devices in the front of the bag.

I have everything I could possibly need packed every single day with me. The smaller the items inside your bag, the better they are. I have my powerful music boxes with me, which are luckily very small but mighty.

I love using my Philips shaver because it is electronic and I have options for trimming or shaving or shaping my beard, plus I can do this without recharging for two weeks. I also love the Sonicare toothbrush from Philips because it's not bigger than a big pen and it stays charged for a couple of weeks, which means I can travel without its charger if I am doing a short trip.

Some of my must-haves are my iPad, my suit, which I typically wear in order to save space, plus some underwear and some shirts, and that is it.

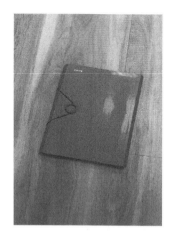

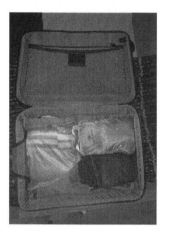

Charge All Your Devices At Night

Always charge all your devices in the evening, including the power banks. You must be always ready to work and have all the tools you need to work, including an iPad, notebook or computer – whatever you work on – as well as a fully charged phone and emergency powerbanks.

Chapter 7
The Network System

Create A Network Checklist

Create a list of the connections you have in your community. How connected are you with your network? If you had an emergency, could you pick up the phone and have people come running to rescue you if you had a financial or health emergency situation? How many of them would do that?

Your network depth as well as width matters. How many meaningful relationships have you created in your network? How many networks or communities are you impacting?

Grow Your Network

Find a creative way to develop new relationships and stay in touch with friends and acquaintances. There needs to be a consistent approach to developing new deep relationships. For example, if you want to increase your network by an extra one thousand people, you only need to meet roughly three extra people per day in a year.

You are only six degrees of separation from the next person you want to meet. There is nothing preventing you from meeting or being in business with the people you want, except for your own creativity and imagination. I routinely create a checklist of who I want to be in communication with every month.

I then go through the list and put it in a relevant sequence of who I want to connect with first, second and third. Then I start connecting with the first person on the list. Find a way to easily stay in touch with the people you want to be related with.

Share something regarding what you are doing and what you need help with and you will discover that a new opportunity opens up as a result of that sharing you did with that person. You could get introduced to something or someone new who could, in turn, create a new door of opportunity for you.

For example, I was out of communication with a friend of mine for a few months. I shared with him that I needed to meet some football managers for some communities in Ghana I am helping to create sustainable businesses for, and he knew a good friend he could put me in touch with.

Just for being in touch with my friend, I now have access to another person in my network. The point of the story is that it is important to create opportunities and possibilities and to complete conversations you put off for a long time, as they all lead to a future you never imagined.

Create A Worldwide Network

As you are travelling stay open-minded and be kind to everyone, from the maid to the porter to the receptionist of the hotel you stay in, or any other person that you meet. You never know who that person is and how they can help you.

Sometimes if you are very nice to the hotel staff they allow you to check out late, at 3 p.m. instead of at 12 p.m., which tends to be the usual time for checkouts. Chat to people you don't know from the airplane or the train so you can create a network of people who can support you everywhere, so you never end up being stranded.

Whenever I travel I prepare by getting to know people from that particular country in social networks so I can be helped in that particular country in case of an emergency. I always have someone I can turn to for information or for help. I recently met someone from Romania, Russia and Belarus in a co-working space.

The conversation I had with them opened up a really good travel opportunity to these countries. I am quite blessed to have inherited my great communication skills from my grandma, who inspired me greatly with how connected she was to the whole world.

It doesn't take me a long time to see which people are open for communication or not.

Start With Small Talk

One of the best techniques to build rapport with new people I meet is to try as much as possible to be fully present in their world and in their reality. I do this by LISTENING attentively about the culture of the other person and I absorb every word they say.

I do my best to be 100% present for what they are really trying to tell me. I am very open to anyone regardless of their religion, faith or any background they may have. One of the best questions to ask to start a conversation is:

"Where are you from?", or perhaps you could make a comment about the weather. I am especially open with people who share similar values of integrity, honesty, openness and kindness.

Smile

Whilst traveling in Bali I met a guy who looked like he was on holiday. He was so relaxed, looking cool and having fun. Turns out he was an Instagrammer earning money with social media videos. By smiling and being kind to him, I had the opportunity to chat to him and get inspired about the lifestyle I wanted to have.

I also met a multimillionaire who shared ways to improve my business with me whilst there, which was actually pretty awesome. Another cool place to meet people worldwide is actually whilst on the plane. You can meet really interesting people and if you have a long haul flight you may have a lot of time to kill anyway.

People like to do business with people they like. The best way to be liked instantly is to put on your best smile and be genuinely kind. You will find that you will attract people to you like a magnet.

Take The Initiative

I used to always be upset when people used to say I had a nice smile, but now I realise this is one of my gifts. As you walk through any railway station, you'll find people are upset. Just smile at them and you will find their reaction will be interesting and you may even start a new friendship or relationship.

Show Genuine Interest In Others

The reason why it is easy for me to make new connections is because I show genuine excitement about other lifestyles and cultures. I look for ways to build rapport by finding things we have in common. I then suggest connecting on

Facebook and, if the person wants, we make a concrete follow up.

Make A Concrete Appointment

What most people do when they meet someone is end their conversation with "let's stay in touch", or "let's meet again sometime", but that is the worst thing you can do – unless you are just being polite and you don't ever want to see the person again.

A better way to cement new friendships and relationships is to make a concrete meet-up for a particular date so you can meet that particular person in a more relaxed way without all the noise of the party you may have met the person at. You may say you know lots of people, but how many people do you really know deep down?

Put Your Friends' Birthdays In Your Calendar

Remember to congratulate them on their special day and send them a card if possible. Try to catch up with them for their birthday, at a minimum.

Send Thank You Cards

Keep a couple of small thank you cards with you so you can hand them to the person who helped you unexpectedly. A small card can have a huge impact on someone who will feel your deep appreciation for them.

Make A Note Of The Person's Name In Your Address Book

Have you ever had that situation where someone texts you but you don't remember who they are? You need a consistent standardised system for how you make notes regarding the person you have just met. Put the person in your phone's address book immediately, as soon as you have met him or her, and write notes regarding where you met them.

Write some hashtags at the bottom of the person's details in your address book, so that you would know how to look for them. For example, you can put a hashtag of what the person does at the bottom (#author, #consultant, #stress coach), a hashtag of the location or the event you met at (#networking night), and a hashtag of what the person was interested in (#business growth).

Take a photo with the person so you can put it in your address book alongside their details. Place that person's birthday there, also.

Create A Networking List

Let's say you attend a conference or a networking party where forty people give you their contact details. It may happen that they give you their phone number, their email, their Facebook ID or their business card. What you don't want is to enter their details in any of your address books and then forget about who they were or what their names were.

That's the purpose of the inbox checklist in your One Life, One List system. When you are in a meeting with so many people, you don't have time to fill in your address book correctly. So, first of all, put the name of the person in your inbox checklist as a new item on the list. You can also create a specific sublist for this purpose.

In that case you have already pre-clustered the information (see the template below). To put the information into the list, use a notation that is easy and quick. I recommend, if at all possible, that you put the name and telephone number immediately into your address book, then call the other person immediately to confirm it's the correct number.

After that, if possible, take a selfie with that person or get a picture of the person immediately. Put that picture in the address book. Make a short note of what you've been talking about with this person or what this person was interested in. You can try using the voice-to-speech functionality on your smartphone.

But finally, the most efficient way is just to put the name and telephone number in your inbox list and a very short description of the content of your conversation. You can take care of everything else after the event. After the event, the first thing you should do is to work on your list and put all your names in your address book, if you have not done that already.

Then, immediately get in touch with those people to create your follow-up conversation meet-up date. Otherwise, each of your contacts remains just that – a contact – rather than a reliable source of collaboration, future business or friendship.

This is the perfect customer relationship management system without using a complex system:

Chapter 8
The Travel System

Prepare For Travel

Find out local means of travel, for example local apps, with options to travel by tube, bus, or aeroplane. When I am in Indonesia I need to download in advance the GoTech app or the Uber app for taking taxis so that I am ready. Register the accounts in advance for the local ways to travel because abroad it is much easier to get stranded.

Keep A Checklist For Particular Countries

Create a travel template checklist for anything you could possibly need, from food, water, hotels, recommended tourist sites, adaptors, local traditions and laws. Maintain the data of your previous journeys there. When a friend of mine wants to go to Indonesia, it doesn't take me a huge amount of time to share my network with him.

Collect a big amount of data about that country, so then you can become an expert in that country. I can share what you need to do if you go there. I can recommend some local friends and they may give you a discount, also. I can share from my travel experience what apps you need, what things you need to take care of or be aware of.

Respect Local Laws

Become familiar with local habits, traditions and laws: for example, in certain countries it is not permissible to drink alcohol in public. In other countries you cannot kiss someone in public, as you can end up in prison. Understand what is forbidden to have on your phone. Find out if the stuff you have on your phone is legal or if it may land you in prison.

When you go to countries where they respect Sharia law, for example, it is forbidden to have any nakedness or porn videos or anything like that on your phone.

Avoid Being Duped

In certain countries you need to be extremely careful in order to avoid having someone put drugs into your luggage. Never use luggage that is not yours. Watch your luggage at all times and take care of it, especially on the plane, where you may fall asleep and people may steal or put something in your luggage.

When I go to Bali I remove everything from my luggage and I clean it thoroughly. If you smoke weed you may be detected. Empty the whole luggage and get rid of all the dust and repack it afterwards. Compress your luggage so that it doesn't take much space.

I use a strong Tumi suitcase into which I insert ten flexible and durable plastic containers, which I purchased separately. These containers act like separators as they enable me to see clearly each item of clothing. Each container is used for a particular item of clothing, and has two zips.

The first zip is used to close the container and the second zip is for compressing the items so they don't take much space. I love packing like this because it means I know exactly where each piece of clothing is, plus they don't get wet and they are safe because the container bags are waterproof.

There are some things which always remain in my suitcase, such as adaptors and other things. I only refresh the things I have to change, such as underwear or other clothes.

I strongly recommend Tumi luggage – they are not fashionable, but the luggage is very comfortable to use because it has a great design and is high quality.

Chapter 9
The Emergency System

Create An Emergency Passport

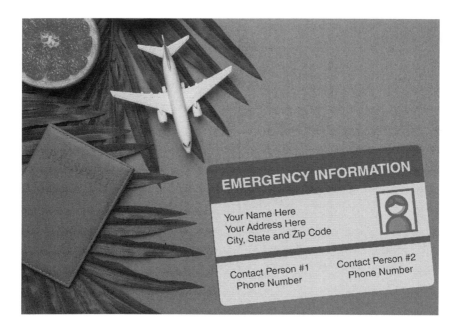

Be aware of what to do in case of an emergency, especially if you have an illness. Prepare for situations like losing your passport or having an accident, needing to be checked in to the hospital for surgery, being robbed in the streets, losing your credit cards, losing all your money or getting hurt.

There may be several situations to be prepared for, such as getting into trouble with someone or being arrested for kissing someone in the street. Always carry with you some notes if you have particular illnesses such as diabetes.

Ideally, you should have an "emergency passport", which is a copy of that same thing. Keep it next to your actual passport inside your backpack. You should also compile a small list, including the telephone number of your doctor or someone to contact in case of an emergency, plus the type of medication you take, along with the dosage.

Put a copy of that in your wallet and in two places inside your backpack, so that if a stranger were to find you unconscious after a potential accident, that person could save your life without struggling to find your details.

Download the emergency template here:
www.thechristianmoser.com/templates

In case you get arrested by the police, establish who can get you out. Make sure you have contingency cash and financial backup. You need to know which cards work in that country and fill your cards with enough reserve cash.

Make An Emergency Checklist

Make a note of where the embassy is. Have your medicine ready. Place it in two places so that if one suitcase or backpack gets lost, you still have the other one. Have enough medicine for seven days, in case of emergencies. Check that you are allowed to take that medicine into that country. In United Arab Emirates, for example, HIV is banned so you wouldn't be able to enter the country if you had it.

Chapter 10
The Security System

One reason why I am always free to go anywhere I like at a moment's notice is because I have all the security documents I could possibly need stored in a secure copy in the cloud. I have my whole life stored in one place, in folders and subfolders which are clearly labelled and easily reachable. I keep all data in one encrypted central file, which means I always feel safe and everything is easily accessible.

One important category I have in the cloud is called "documents", and inside that I have subcategories where I put my ID card, and all the information inside my ID; for example, the number, the issue date, the expiry date. I also have the password for the Wi-Fi router or any other details I need easily accessible.

I have the data for my passport number and all other details inside the passport for easy copying and pasting. I also keep the registration numbers of all my documents alongside PINs and passwords for various online subscriptions, because that keeps me sane. I give everything a clear label in the cloud so I can easily find it later and even work from bed.

When I need my passport in order to make a reservation I have all the data with me on my computer or iPad and I don't need to go to my backpack to check the details. It is dangerous if someone gets access to your details, of course, so be careful, as you are responsible for this list. I keep a list of flight and hotel membership programmes I am enrolled in, and I try to leverage the membership as much as possible for possible perks, discounts and time in VIP lounges.

Data in the "documents list" may make you a vulnerable target should someone get the file. Be careful not to leave all the data printed. You can take measures so the data is encrypted.

Chapter 11
The Office System

Systemising your work can take a lot of time initially but it will lead to huge long-term payoffs. Since I keep about 90% of work files digitally in the cloud in an organised way I am able to have access to my data, my workflow or information about clients easily, when I need it and wherever I need it.

Have A Paperless Office

I scan everything using the Office Lens application, then I store my papers in digital archives. When I need to be creative, I draw my ideas on paper first. I typically write down all my ideas on the office flip chart or on colourful Post-it notes that I arrange on boards. It's a good idea to pin the project to the wall until it is finished, since it is easier to move stuff around there.

Once I'm happy that it is complete, I scan everything to the cloud. The Office Lens app is great for recreating digitally whatever flip chart you are doing and it makes it look perfect.

Chapter 12
The Stack System

This system is a fantastic system to get stuff done in the office. When I started to work with that philosophy the stack of papers I had to do was full and now it is empty, because I am so much more productive than before. The stack is an efficient way to organise all the issues you are working on that require paperwork to be submitted, notes or documents related to a particular task to be looked at or bills to be paid.

Your goal should be to find solutions for and get rid of all your paperwork.

Standardise Your Filing System

The most important thing is to first standardise your filing system so that all paperwork you process for each part of the system is available in the same format. Whenever you receive some paperwork, immediately put all those papers belonging to the same thing into one plastic file. Always use the same size file; in Germany we usually use DIN A4.

The impact on you is that you have clarity and a clear view of all the items, but also can transport the documents whenever you need them somewhere else. So, whenever I travel, in most cases I just take out the *Backlog*, *Next*, and *Work In Progress* files, put them into my mobile folder, and I'm ready to perform.

So what you need is just filing boxes, clear view plastic folders of the same size, some labels for the boxes, and a transport cover for when travelling. You also need knowledge about how to apply this system to your workflow and you need to apply it consistently.

Here are the elements of the stack:

The Stack: a stacked collection of boxes.

Inbox: whatever comes in, put it there first.

The Single-Item File: a plastic file which always has the same size, where you put in all the stuff belonging to the current item.

The Mobile Folder: this is a thick folder of 1 or 2 cm that you

INBOX

BACKLOG

NEXT

WIP

ON-HOLD

ARCHIVE

can put all the standardised plastic files you might need into when you travel.

Backlog: all the things you work on anytime.

Next: the things you want to do next.

WIP: the work-in-process folder is for things you are working on today or currently.

On-Hold: the things you have already done but are waiting for someone else for the next step.

Archive: all that has been completed and might be archived digitally or dumped in the bin.

Bin: the final destination for everything you will never need again.

Digital Archive: things you might need again at some time in the future, but for which the work has been completed.

Just use the labels above. Print them out and apply them to your boxes!

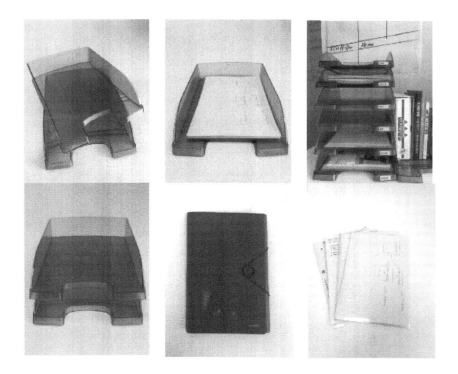

Organise Your Workflow

This is the workflow I use. Feel free to add or take away any of the workflow elements according to your way of working. But, once you have perfected your system, **use it under all circumstances** so you can easily systemise your business.

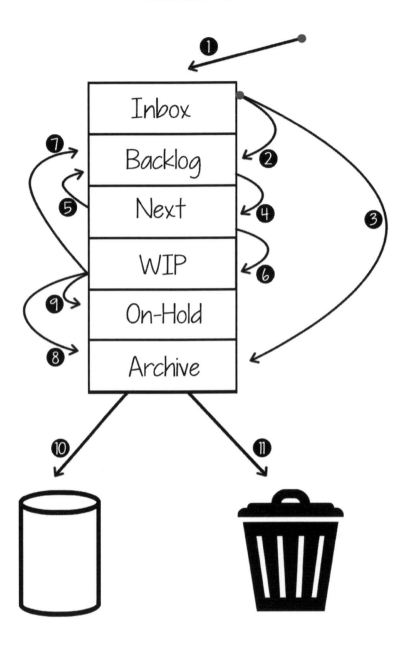

1) Paper comes in. Just put it in the top box labelled **Inbox**. Also, communicate to everybody that everything that is for you should always and only be placed there!

2)   Decide whether the current item is something you are going to work on. If the answer is yes, put it into the **Backlog** box.

3)   If you decide that the current item doesn't need to be worked on at all, put it in the **Archive** box.

4)   Whilst you don't plan to work on something, leave it in the **Backlog** box, otherwise move it to the **Next** box.

5)   It might happen that you decide not to work on an item in the **Next** box for the moment. Put it back into your **Backlog** box.

6)   If you plan to work on something today, put it into the **Work-In-Process** box.

7)   If you change your mind and decide to work on that paperwork another time, move it back to your **Backlog** box.

8)   Once you have completed the work on that paperwork, then put it into the **Archive** box.

9) Put paperwork that needs the help, reply or authorisation of others into the **On-Hold** box until you receive the result.

10) Decide if you still want to keep the paperwork. Scan it to your digital archive and place it, labelled, in the correct folder if you want to keep the paperwork digitally.

11) If everything is done and you will never need the paperwork again, then dump it.

Standardise Your Files

Besides all the items I manage with my system, I have some standard files for standard items.

The Due-File: Here I put in all invoices I have to pay urgently.

The Archive-File: this is the place for all the small stuff to be archived, besides single files of already concluded items.

The 2Read-File: this is where I keep articles I print out and want to read anytime.

The Receipt-File: when travelling for business I pay for various things, and I always keep all the new receipts with me in one folder, compartmentalised into subfolders. I collect these immediately after my return into a file, so that they are available for the bookkeeping in case some of them are tax deductible.

I carry with me these folders: **The Due-File, The Archive-File, The Receipt-File,** and whenever I get to my office I give all my receipts to my assistant. He assigns them immediately to the credit card or bank account invoices. I always go through those standard folders so they are emptied as quickly as possible.

The ultimate goal is to work with as little paper as possible. As soon as a file has gone through the process it disappears from your stack, and also from your One Life, One List checklist on your PC or notebook.

Here is a checklist of papers you can typically throw:

"What To Throw" Checklist

❖ Guide manuals (you typically can find these online anyway).

❖ Receipts after scanning them.

❖ Private receipts after they are paid.

❖ Dump everything you don't have to keep.

"What To Keep" Checklist:

❖ Testimonials.

❖ Papers for the authorities.

❖ Insurance policies.

❖ Contracts.

❖ Company registration documents.

❖ Power of attorney documents.

❖ Documents pertaining to you owning your house.

❖ Your will.

❖ Business receipts.

❖ Nostalgia box.

What is the nostalgia box? When I started to declutter my life, I realised that I wanted to keep certain sentimental things and I don't ever want to throw them away. For example, the old photos of my son, or the invoice I got when my son was born, which reminds me of that evening. Once a year I go through this box – and sometimes I throw some things even from there .

Print Out Your Notes

Work on paper during the day if you prefer by first preparing all your to-do lists for the day then printing them out so you can physically tick off your to-dos or cross them out on your paper with a highlighter pen.

Chapter 13
The Notation System

Notations and abbreviations help to simplify your life and save you time. Notations are used for effective typing. You can invent your own notation at any time. In **One Life, One List** we use our own notation and continuously improve on it.

I use the notation system to shorten the process when I enter new things in my calendar, such as dates, locations, names, to-do lists, projects to be done or projects delegated. I use the same identical system when I write notes on paper.

This is really useful when I am learning new things at conferences or events because there is usually not much time for that, and also because it is more important to write down the actionable steps that you will implement rather than just be astounded by what you have learnt and do absolutely nothing with the information when you go back to work the next day.

The Calendar Notation System

When I have an appointment, I immediately place the important information in my calendar for that exact date and time, and I also write in the specific task that I want to discuss with that person. For example, I put a bracket on the date "August 10, 2019, 9:00AM, Call Lily on WhatsApp [+00000000], Discuss [Book Structure]". I write the specifics so that I will not miss the important matters.

If you do that, you will feel in control of your time because you are managing your time well by immediately making a note of the important details, never feeling lost or wasting time to remember what you were supposed to do later on. This is how my calendar looks when using that notation:

The Format

Format	Examples
What [With whom]@Where:Details	Book[Lily]@Whatsapp: Defining Skeleton

The Conference Notation System

Below is how a typical paper looks when I take notes during a consultation session or conference. I always use the same notation system to make sure that I never forget anything, will do all the tasks coming up and will save all the information I got and will have clarity about all the questions I have.

I typically make a circle around the person who organised the meeting. When I get a piece of information, I draw a square when there is a task to do.

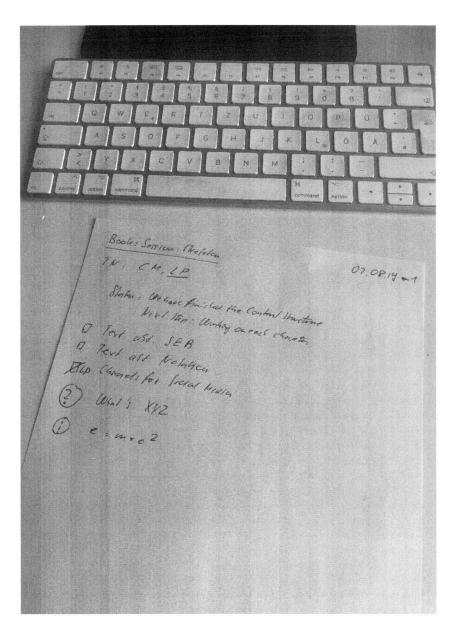

 xy

TN: CM, <u>LP</u>

Project: Subject: Detail

DD.MM.YY - #

~~DD.MM.YY - #~~

The Notations

Element	Explanation
☐	A to-do which is still to be done.
◩ xy	A to-do which is already delegated to the person mentioned next to it. I use initials, usually (CM = Christian Moser).
⊠	A to-do which is done or has been transferred to another list.
ⓘ	Important and remarkable information or an insight.
⊘?	Something which was unclear to me.

TN: CM, <u>LP</u>	The participants (TN=teilnehmer, which is the German word for participants). The underlined one is the organiser of the meeting or session.
Project: Subject: Detail	Description of the topic.
DD.MM.YY - #	Date and page number.
~~DD.MM.YY - #~~	Whenever I have fully completed my notes, having done or transferred all my to-dos, I mark it in this way so that I know that this paper is ready to archive or dump.

How To Find Everything Easily

Never archive your WhatsApp or Messenger history, since you will need that to remind you of previous conversations you had with various people. I have all my emails in my archive and I can easily look for a keyword or the name of the sender to find what I need because the search mechanisms of Apple are really excellent.

I moved all my emails and my videos to my Apple Cloud and I am using only 10% of the space. I have all my WhatsApp chats there and I regularly do backups. I use G Suite with unlimited space because that allows me to have my business email forwarded to my gmail, and to send business emails using my gmail. It also allows me to store and easily share a lot of data using Google Drive.

If I need to find the pictures of a certain person then I can immediately have that available because I have each photo I have ever taken in the cloud. The face detection scans determine who the person is, if you have tagged the photo one time, and from there you can be automatically identified in all the photos with a similar face.

This algorithm is present everywhere and it makes searching for photos much easier. I love using the cloud because as soon as I search for any document, I can trace it immediately by keyword and I can see the date also. I used to carry a lot of documents whilst travelling worldwide, but then I had an aha moment in my life, during the last year, when I discovered that all the paperwork I was carrying with me around the world all the time was not necessary.

I was in Bali at the time. I scanned everything with the Office Lens software on my iPhone, I put the files in my digital archive and I destroyed all the paperwork, as you can see in the picture. What I've discovered since then is that I've never needed to use any one of those scanned documents, but it's great to have them all handy and accessible in my digital archive, just in case I do need them.

I took that photo whilst in Bali to be reminded of that insight. I finally refined the concept so much that I hardly ever carry any paperwork on me thanks to the "paperless office" idea.

Use Simple Efficiency Boosters

I have created a checklist of Simple Efficiency Boosters (SEB) that cost little but help you to have a huge impact to simplify your life:

The "Simple Efficiency Boosters" are a **simple** thing or action which has a huge impact on your productivity in return for the time or money you have to invest in it.

If you are like me, perhaps you have inspiring goals. But do you ever suffer setbacks that stop you from achieving those goals? Sometimes those setbacks could be easily prevented with small but very clever strategies that save you time, energy and keep you from endless frustration.

They are not spectacular in design or appearance, but they are multipurpose; some of them might be already known, but not fully taken advantage of in our daily life.

• Carry toothpicks with you because they are absolutely great for cleaning earphones and also your fingernails, without hurting them, and they cost nothing. When my AirPods are dirty I can't hear through them and that has a huge impact on my business. Always carry spare AirPods, or have a toothpick so you can clean them effectively.

• Get used to the speech-to-text functionality of your smartphone, whether it is Siri, Alexa, or any other app. You save a lot of time when sending text messages or writing emails and text. When you speak another language, get used to speaking in that language.

• Always double check the message you are sending before pressing "send". You may waste a lot of time explaining incorrect messages sent using predictive text, and you may end up in serious arguments with the receiver of the message, too!

• Use the mobile data button to deactivate all the apps sending you messages. Also deactivate wireless Internet so that people can reach you by the simple normal telephone function or SMS, but so that you are otherwise able to work in peace and quiet.

- When you have finished an appointment, set your timer to the next one immediately. Even though, for example, the next telephone conference might be five minutes later and your calendar has already reminded you, you might get distracted and forget it.

- Don't use voice recordings when sharing something important because you can't listen to voicemail during a meeting and you can't see what has been said when scrolling through your messages, so whenever you have to share something important use text writing.

- Get a small gadget to wind up the earphone cables so you can keep them tidy. It takes a lot of time to untangle knotted cables.

- Even though you might use Bluetooth earphones, have a cabled set always ready. If you participate in a long conference, the battery of your earphones might run out of power, therefore you can switch to the cabled earphones.

- If you work internationally, always be clear on the time zones when making appointments. Either refer to GMT, UTC or agree to one specific time zone when talking with others. Be always aware of the time differences between the zones you are in touch with and use your smartphone app to list those.

• Always have with you a little block of Post-it notes and a pen. This is the most effective thing when batteries are empty and you need to make notes.

• Always schedule appointments with a buffer time of fifteen minutes before, and after the next appointment as well.

• Always have a package of nuts and glucose with you, especially when you are attending very long events.

• Standardise literally everything you do, regardless of the business you are in. Use (DIN-A4) plastic sleeves to place together all your paperwork for further processing.

• Use the macro function of your notebook or smartphone to create shortcuts or notations for important things you always need (e.g. PPN for passport number), so whenever you fill out your check-in for the next flight you have the number ready and don't need to take out your passport.

- Find the best format to make notes and give it a structure. I prefer simple plain printer paper since this is always available and it is easy to archive afterwards.

- Share simple yet effective strategies for automating your business with others. Some things you know may be very basic and common sense to you, but may be very useful to others who are not aware of them. I had two free coaching sessions today and I became filled with joy seeing how ecstatic people are sometimes to learn the simplest things, like how to collaborate on the same document using free tools such as Google Drive.

Chapter 14
The Income Tracker System

Many people fail as entrepreneurs despite taking so much training and doing many great courses because they don't have a way to manage their life after the events they attend, so they go back to their usual life without making many changes. Instead of that I have figured out a great way to build in accountability to your life so you can get more done.

The key aspect of that is promising to manage a particular part of your life, such as your finances, by a certain date. It is great to promise to do something, but ask yourself, by when will you do it? I use my version of an income tracker system invented by T. Harv Eker and I have simply added the element of accountability to that system by adding a way to manage my promises and track my money.

I am not a financial advisor, but the principle of the income tracker system can have an impact on every area of your life because, as you become more efficient, you will find that you will be able to potentially create more wealth, maintain better relationships and have comfort and ease in your life.

Imagine what it would feel like to be told by your supplier that you didn't make a payment, and having to pay again because you could not find the receipt. Imagine the kind of losses you could incur if this was something that happened on a recurring basis.

Imagine if you had different standing orders for many things and you simply paid them without checking your account – you could end up spending a lot of money and not even realising.

Make A Log Of Your Expenditure

Download your bank statements in Excel then start tracking all the money you have incoming, and all the money you have spent, then divide your outgoings into "necessary", "waste" and "special treat". Was what you purchased something you wanted or something you needed? If you track everything you will find it easier to save money.

I am very careful with my budgeting and planning. As a savvy money manager, I know it's not only what I make that is important , but also what I keep. You can create your own Excel spreadsheet tracking your money and you can calculate the things you spend on that are not necessities. For example, if you are a smoker and you smoke ten packs of cigarettes, it's not a need, but a want.

When I started doing this I became aware of all the money I was wasting by doing a calculation at the end of the month. I noticed I used to spend five euros for coffee daily despite having the option of bringing my own coffee from home. On top of it, there is a coffee machine at my workplace.

I used to always choose the easy option of simply buying expensive coffee from my favourite cafe, but I am now more aware of the compounding effect of reducing my expenses and keeping more of my hard-earned cash.

The Self-Organisation Principle

Taking the decision to becoming organised is the core of making this system work. If you are organised you can make all the below systems work. Otherwise if you continue leaving things everywhere then it will be impossible for you to enjoy this system fully and use it to the maximum potential.

Chapter 15
The Excellent Habits System

Discipline is the number one key to achieving productivity. There are some things we all know we should do, yet we don't, such as drinking two litres of water or having eight hours of sleep each day.

People sometimes get stressed or get a panic attack when they are running out of time to finish their tasks, resulting in headaches, bad moods or even blaming others when, in fact, it is the result of just being so laid-back, or the result of poor planning.

Following a certain programme is a great way to get things done. Excellent habits can enable you to be more efficient and more effective. This system helps me to get organised and obtain great results for my coaching clients. This system is based on the BE – DO – HAVE system.

In order to achieve and have what you want, you need initially to take the actions you need to get there. But even before that, you need to be or become a certain person in order to take those actions. For example, if you are or you believe you are a procrastinator, then you are likely to do nothing, and to have nothing, or close to nothing, of what you want.

If you change that belief with "I am a powerful, courageous, extraordinary leader" then the actions you take will be those of a powerful leader. Then ask yourself: "What would a powerful leader do?"

What kind of habits would a powerful leader have on a daily basis as part of his or her routine? You then choose to do those actions as part of the excellent habits system in accordance with the person you are. Make a list of the kinds of habits and routines a powerful leader will have, and choose to do those things on a daily, weekly, monthly basis, or whatever the case for you, depending on your particular goal.

For example, to become a master in any skill, whether it is public speaking, IT consulting or anything else, you need to practice for about 10,000 hours. Studies have shown that you typically need to do something for at least 21 days in order to get that habit ingrained in your routine, in the same way you always brush your teeth every day.

The first few days will be harder, but as time goes by things will become easier. The important thing is choosing those routines that you know will get you to where you want to be. It is also extremely important to follow the BE – DO – HAVE system, because otherwise your to-do lists will look completely different.

If you believe you are courageous, you will take bold actions. If you focus on the feeling of not being good enough, of being afraid, or on demotivating things you tell yourself, such as "I am lazy", "I am disorganised", "I never do what I want to do", "I feel trapped", "I am bored", then your "DO" list is going to look smaller and very boring, too. That is why it is important to do the "I am" list.

Create your "I am" list, then your "Do" list, which is the Excellent Habits List. Then create your "Have" list. What is it that you really want and need to have?

Write down your "I am" list here:

Choose from this template the items that apply, or create your own. Download the templates list at

www.thechristianmoser.com/templates

"I Am" List

I am powerful

I am bold

I am extraordinary

I am funny

I am intelligent

I am a leader

I am organised

I am loving

I am honest

I am kind

I am interesting

I am educated

I am conscientious

I am adventurous

Then write down your "Do" list, which I like to call The Routine System.

Knowing you are now a powerful, extraordinary leader or whatever it is you wrote in your list, what kind of routines do you choose to do daily? Include those in your "Routine" list.

Follow A Routine

My routine is the main reason why I am still alive and sane today. Being personally successful, healthy, driven, and successful at work is the result of continuous excellent habits I have developed over time, such as eating well, going to the gym three times a week, doing some sort of varied type of exercise once a week on top of that, like swimming, and taking my vitamins and other medication.

Develop A Morning Routine

I schedule various routines for different parts of the day and the week so that I remain joyful and contented. I have routines for what I am doing in the morning. My calendar reminds me to look at my One Life, One List in the morning.

This is what my morning routine looks like:

Morning Routine Checklist:

- drink water
- brush teeth
- apply body lotion
- do morning gym challenge

- plan my day printable sheet
- important projects checklist
- go through "My Promises" list
- listen to a motivational speech

I am at work during the afternoon so I have a work checklist, with sub-checklists for each client I work with. Create your work checklist. This will vary daily, of course.

Create An Evening Routine

For me this is what my routine looks like at approximately 9.30 p.m.:

Evening Routine Checklist:

- social media hour
- read books from my reading stack
- finish all evening tasks already planned
- check I fulfilled my promises from "My Promises" checklist
- check if everything is necessary in my lists
- 1 hour of routines to maintain my list updated

During the planning hour I dedicate each evening, I create a backlog list and a work-in-process jobs list. I always do the prioritised tasks first. I declutter my lists and do daily maintenance of the lists.

Once you have created your routine habits, edit, delete or reschedule what you have done and what you haven't done into the main list in the evening.

Develop A Weekly Routine

I usually try to get everything done based on my simple main template, but from time to time it needs more planning. Sometimes I tend to plan based on weeks when there is too much work. Our One Life, One List framework does not force you to keep your structure forever.

Just adapt it to your needs and, especially with our software, it will be easy to restructure your whole system with a few clicks. With an editor, or an online notepad, you can already do it anyway. Here is an example of my weekly routine:

- **Inbox**
- **Recurring**
  - ○ **Daily**
    - ■ **AllDay**
    - ■ **Morning**
    - ■ **Evening**
  - ○ **Weekly**
    - ■ **Saturday**
- **Promises**
- **Requests**
- **Conversations**
  - ○ **Core**
  - ○ **InFocus**
- **Today**
- **Next**
- **Backlog**
- **Projects**
  - ○ **Project**
    - ■ **WIP**
    - ■ **Backlog**
    - ■ **OnHold**
    - ■ **Team**
    - ■ **Info**

- **Core**
  - ○ **ToBuy**
  - ○ **ToRead**
  - ○ **MyMovies**
  - ○ **MyPosts**
  - ○ **MySayings**
  - ○ **Wisdom**

- o **MyLifeHacks**
- o **MyLinks**
  - ■ **ToCheck**
  - ■ **Area**
  - ■ **Area**
- o **Infobase**

Create A Sprint Routine

A sprint routine is a term I copied from the agile framework I use for project management. I use the term "sprint" which means a limited period of time where I specify what I want to accomplish. You can call it a quarter or semester or whatever you like.

Then I split the sprint into weeks and I specify what I need to do each week by creating a sublist for each day of the week. That way I can already start to plan my tasks very concretely and whenever something comes up for the upcoming weeks I can already insert it there.

Finally, I have a weekly backlog for all the stuff it is not mandatory to have done on a specific day. And, last but not least, I have a sprint backlog for anything which should be done at any time during the whole sprint.

The upcoming One Life, One List software will empower you to enhance your effectiveness while using the reference functionality and I am certain you will love it. But, for the moment, this here is already very helpful.

- **Sprint 1 (01.06.2018 – 07.07.2018)**
  - **Goals**
  - **KW 24 (11.06.2018 – 17.06.2018)**
    - **Wed 11.06.2018**
      - **WIP**
      - **Backlog**
    - **Thu 14.06.2018**
      - **WIP**
      - **Backlog**
    - **Fri 15.06.2018**
      - **WIP**
      - **Backlog**
    - **Sat 16.06.2018**
      - **WIP**
      - **Backlog**
    - **Weekly Backlog**
  - **KW 25 (18.06.2018 – 24.06.2018)**
    - **Weekly Backlog**
  - **KW 26 (25.06.2018 – 01.07.2018)**
    - **Weekly Backlog**
  - **Sprint-Backlog**

The weekly routine typically looks the same Monday to Friday, but on Saturday I have specific things planned in my routine.

Saturday Routine:

- Revise all projects and all lists
- Market shopping
- Barber shop
- Manicure and pedicure
- Laundry

Then write down what you are planning to have in the future. Write a full comprehensive wish list of items you desire, the more specific the better.

Be Your

Word

With Joy And

Ease

Chapter 16
The Accountability System

Create A "My Promises" List

One very useful list I have is called "My Promises". This list contains what I promised, to whom and by when. This enables me to structure my life in such a way that I never forget my promises and I am able to have a system to put in place so that I keep my word.

What tends to happen when you make promises to different people is that you may forget to do what you promised. If you make it a habit to not only write the list, but check the list as part of your daily routine, you are setting yourself up for success. For example, you can write, "I promised Lily to do the video for today", then you write anything you need to do on your list.

Once the app is created, you will be able to also search different tasks related to a particular keyword, a particular date or a particular person. For now, you can simply tick off or cross out the tasks done in your daily planner as that will give you a feeling of satisfaction, knowing you have completed the tasks.

I love creating client checklists as that enables me to visualise how far I have come down the project path and how much time I still need to assign to it. One thing that helped me tremendously in business was this principle I have called 100% **integrity**. Nothing works in your life or your business without integrity.

To be in integrity you need to keep your promises, manage your requests and your conversations and that's it. Every time you make a promise, put that promise in a sublist of promises including when and to whom you made the commitment. Whenever you request something from someone, put that in writing also, in another sublist called "Requests".

Name **who** is the person you are holding accountable and **by when** the person promised to do this. The request needs to be very clear and it needs to be put in writing, because anything that is not written down could be misinterpreted or misheard. You need to have a routine to check regularly on whether the task is being done.

For example, you can request someone to do something by the end of the month, but every week you need to know what has been done. Check what was done against what was promised in the "Promises" list and see which part of the conversation was missing, if there was something that didn't get done.

Another list you need to create is a list of conversations that need to occur in order to achieve the tasks you want done. You can call that list "Conversations".

Chapter 17
The Self-Reflection System

Most entrepreneurs, consultants, coaches, IT programmers or people from any other field of work tend to work very many hours then return to their children and families, and forget to take time for themselves. Sometimes they can no longer cope with the accumulation of stress and they end up mentally ill or with a serious physical illness.

It is all because they didn't take the time to self-reflect on what they really want out of life. As a result, it may take them years and years before they realise they are in a job they hate, or they are no longer passionate about what they do because they are not spending enough time to really listen to their heart.

If this is you, I know exactly how you feel, because I used to feel the same. I had my own moments when I felt lost because I simply could not cope with the death of my daughter. I took therapy and a full year of trying to reconnect with myself and what I really wanted and since then I know this system is crucial for the functioning of all the other systems.

How To Cope With Overwhelm

Imagine waking up in the morning at 5 a.m. As the alarm clock is ringing, you start to hear a voice inside your head. Sometimes it could say: "Hey, today is going to be a good day." Other days it could say: "Hey, today I am so stressed, because I have a client meeting." As you are now awake, you have a choice to substitute negative feelings with great ones.

Nothing gives you more freedom than realising YOU are the creator of the story you tell yourself each day. You can decide how the story starts and you can also decide how the story ends. Whilst you cannot manipulate your circumstances, you can decide today and every day is going to be a happy day, regardless of what happens.

As soon as you see anger, frustration, sadness, a feeling of not being good enough, say "Thank you for sharing," and move on to a new feeling of happiness. You can only be creative when you are happy, contented and you have a free space to create in. You will struggle to be productive when your judgement is clouded by anger or a feeling of being small, not good enough or anything similar.

Every time you are in the spotlight for something you have done or are about to do and there is even a slight chance of being criticised, that may make you feel stressed. However, the only person you should be comparing yourself to is yourself.

Are you better now than you were yesterday? If the answer is yes, realise you don't have to look nice to impress others. Appreciate yourself for the progress you have achieved. Spend a few minutes daily in the morning appreciating what you are grateful for.

Appreciate yourself and anything you have accomplished. Feel the gratitude you have for those around you and for anything you have done. Meditate in order to instil calmness into your mind before you head to the gym or the office. It makes no sense to remain in a bad mood.

Reflect on yourself and give yourself time to think about you. Reflect on how you could do the same things you are currently doing, only better. How could you improve? Be prepared to take your own coaching. Be coachable. I know a year from today I will smile when I analyse how far I have come.

Continuously review and implement better habits in your routine checklists. I may be struggling with certain aspects of my life but I know in a year I will laugh at my struggles. Say sorry to people you have upset or wronged in some way. People appreciate that if you really mean it.

Chapter 18
The Well-Being System

Whilst I am not a personal trainer or well-being coach, I know that unless I have a well-being system that I follow, I won't be able to carry out my checklists of any kind because I won't have the energy to do it. I am a big fan of Rupert Murdoch because he shares about five things successful entrepreneurs do, and one especially impactful thing he said is that, "Whatever you do, be aware you only have ONE body."

He says that whatever you do, your body carries through to the end of your life. So be aware of what you can do for your own body so you do have a long life. I go to the gym four times a week, where I typically do a high-intensity workout for thirty minutes, and I typically get seven hours of sleep, though I am aware that everyone has their own sleep pattern and sleep needs.

I schedule my gym workouts in the calendar like an appointment and I am 100% focused on working out when I am there, without wasting time chatting to people. If you are travelling, I recommend sling trainers when you are in a place where there is no gym.

I have a minimalist kit for the gym which is very light. I can even fold my shoes so they don't take much space and also so that there is no excuse not to work out, even while on long-haul trips to Indonesia. I sometimes go jogging in the morning, I conclude my day with swimming, and I typically implement a morning challenge set by my personal trainer.

These are the sling trainers:

My personal trainer created a great ten-minute workout challenge routine which involves push-ups, though sometimes we change the plan for another one to keep my workouts interesting. I drink freshly squeezed lemon in warm water alongside some Himalayan salt in the morning, in order to get my bowels moving and keep my metabolism active, because my personal trainer recommended this drink to me.

As a result, I feel empowered and full of energy most days. This workout is a simple efficiency booster, as it is one of the small things I do that has an immense impact on my life and my productivity. You don't need to live like a monk, but if you are ready to simplify your life you will feel an added sense of relief and flexibility.

Reduce Or Get Rid Of Your Addictions

Addictions to sugar, alcohol, cigarettes, or even binge-watching Netflix movies has an impact on your health and wealth. Decide to reduce or get rid of some of these addictions in order to feel fitter and enhance your energy.

Chapter 19
The Wisdom System

Have you ever been so inspired by someone's words that you doubled your productivity that day? Personal motivation has a direct impact on the results you get at work, how long a task takes to complete, as well as the efficiency and effectiveness of the task.

That is why I have made it a habit to collect the insights, shares, and sayings that have impressed me over the years. Every time I hear something spectacular I write it down on my "Wisdom" list. The Wisdom system is something I use to take immediate notes of anything that has an impact on me, so that when I am feeling low I can read it and feel inspired. I created one section in the Wisdom list called "Insights", where I record links to websites that inspire me.

Each part called "Insights" has sublists also, with particular items I have learnt from various people that I am planning to implement in my life. For example, I got the insight from T. Harv Eker about the money tracker system he has, which recommends using six jars in order to divide money into various categories for better management.

Because of this I am now managing my money in a much more effective way and I also have a scheduled way to give to charity and invest in myself and my own learning. I keep a separate Wisdom Diary, where I journal regarding what happens with my day.

I note what emotional experiences I had, what I was thinking, how I was dealing with that situation. I extract as much wisdom as I can by reflecting on my thoughts later on. It's important to have that wisdom digitally so you can search for it and you can grow by reflecting on your moments of wisdom.

As long as you write your thoughts down on paper or digitally, you can have access to your wisdom easily when you need it. I also have a separate daily technical diary where I make notes of technical insights I had and ways I was able to overcome problems at work and come up with creative solutions.

I also love using this system for collecting any wisdom I receive from others, such as quotes of famous people I see in social media, on YouTube, or any other phrases I hear from people around me. I save those pieces of wisdom into a "Wisdom" list, to refer to as part of my routine of getting inspired and motivated.

I also have a list for things I would like to include in my social media posts – different keywords and strategies for sharing my message.

Chapter 20
The Relationship Management System

This system is about how to create a work-life balance so you can spend more time with your family and friends. Since I am currently single, I live fully the luxury minimalism principle, but if your partner loves hoarding things you may have to come up with a compromise.

Your partner may not like luxury minimalism, which is okay. You can pick and choose the principles from this book that suit your personal life. You may have a very large house and you may have all the space you want to put whatever you want in it.

If you are both different in terms of your preferences, find a middle way so you don't hurt each other and don't get angry about each other. Find a way to recommend and show the benefit of living in luxury minimalism to your partner if this is something you prefer.

Try not to complain – find a compromise. Learn to live harmoniously with your partner or get out of the relationship. Don't try to fix others – find a common way to live. I found my way of living that makes me happy and I am ready to accept others with their way of life.

Make a compromise if you need to use shared space. Explain your principles and enrol your partner in the same principles or values. For example, for me, being punctual is ultra-important. If you find yourself in conflict with your partner, keep calm and don't take rash decisions.

Sleep Before Taking Difficult Decisions

Chapter 21
The Balance System

One of the hardest things I have been eager to create as an entrepreneur is a feeling of emotional balance. I continuously have peaks and troughs in my mood because of things that occur to me at work or in my personal life, but thanks to the Balance System I continuously manage my mood through meditation, personal transformation and self-reflection.

I have a routine which helps me bounce back into action and manage my emotional life when I am feeling down. Here are some ideas you can implement in your life: listen to classical music, meditate, practice feeling happy for no reason at all.

There are certain things that always put a smile on my face. The greatest thing of all is that they don't need to be big things. Small things I do to treat myself include having an organised house, a nice cup of my favourite coffee or spending a few great moments with my friends.

I try my best to be happy within myself, and I love my lists – they give me a feeling of freedom, especially because I can meet my son anytime and anywhere. Regardless of your role in the family, whether you are a father, mother or partner, it is important to keep a good balance when it comes to spending time with your family.

I hope you will implement at least some of these organisational tips so you, too, can enjoy a life of freedom and choice.

Chapter 22
The Community System

The One Life, One List philosophy is based on the concept of collaboration. As you start creating checklists, templates, cheat sheets for the processes you need to do in your life or business to get organised, you develop systems that other people could also follow or improve on.

Customise this system for you or your business and you will then be able to share that with the community of other freedom lifestyle business owners, expats, consultants, and stay-at-home mums around the world.

Everybody could potentially use, improve or add features or items to your customised system and you could share your experience or your systems with others open source, which will give freedom to others to contribute to your creativity.

Share Freely What You Have Created

The great part about this system is that it is fully customisable to you. You also have the option of becoming a creator in the system and have full control over whether you would like to share your checklists with others or not.

This is your list and your data and you can share what you want. You can exchange ideas and stuff with others, then easily integrate other people's checklists into your system and advance much faster in whatever you are doing.

In a normal business or life there is a lot of time wasted learning an efficient and effective system for getting something done. With this solution you can skip over years and years of trial and error if someone was to simply share with you pieces of knowledge you don't currently have that are going to fill the missing puzzle in your life or business.

Chapter 23
The 31-Day One Life, One List Organisation Challenge

How many times have you heard about a fantastic system for organising your life and your business, yet you simply read it then thought to yourself, *wow, what a great system*, then went back to your normal life and did nothing at all with it?

That's precisely why I have created the **31-Day One Life, One List Organisation Challenge** for anyone wanting more out of life.

Maybe you are sick and tired of being sick and tired.

Maybe you have had enough of the clutter and mess that isn't allowing you to be as productive as you know you can be.

Maybe you are ready to start afresh.

Maybe you are ready to double your productivity or create more.

Perhaps you are going through a divorce, your kids are going away to university, or who knows what other reason you have to do this.

Join the movement of other entrepreneurs wanting freedom in their lives by doing the 31-day challenge. I do realise this system may take some time to implement. As a busy person, it is inevitable that your work is going to be the main obstacle for getting yourself organised. However if you do things bit by bit you will find they will become easier.

31-Day Challenge:

1. Buy Essentials For Decluttering.
2. Create An Empty Space In An Area Of Your Office Or House.
3. Separate Items Into: Items To Keep, Giveaway/Charity Box, Recycle, Rubbish, Receipts, Archive.
4. Separate Office Work Documents Using The Stack System.
5. Organise The Same Area Into Labelled Containers Or Dividers.
6. Buy Anything That Will Turn That Area Into Your Perfect Area.
7. Give Away Unwanted Clothes Or Other Items To Charity.

8. Recycle What Is Possible.

9. Separate Your Receipts By Categories.

10. Archive What's No Longer Important.

11. Create Your One Life, One List.

12. Organise Your To-Do List Into Sublists By Type.

13. Create Your "My Promises" List With Subcategories: Promises, Requests And Conversations.

14. Create Your "Excellent Habits" List For Your Morning, Evening And Weekend Routine.

15. Track What You Are Spending Your Time On.

16. Reduce Time Spent Ineffectively And Replace That Time With Productive Activities.

17. Create Your "Luxury Lifestyle Wish List" And Itemise Which Luxury Items You Will Invest In.

18. Schedule Your Shopping.

19. Schedule Your Weekly Luxury Experiences.

20. Create Your Luxury Minimalist Wardrobe.

21. Create Your Minimalist Room.

22. Create Your " Ready To Go" Backpack.

23. Create Your "Ready To Go" Suitcase.

24. Create Your Emergency Passport.

25. Create Your Security List.

26. Schedule Time With Family.

27. Expand And Connect With Your Network.

28. Track Your Money With The Income Tracker.

29. Create Your Notation List And Update Your Phone Notation System.

30. Create Your Self-Reflection, Wisdom, Relationship And Balance Routine.

31. Work Out And Raise Your Energy.

Stay in touch with other fabulous entrepreneurs who are creating a freedom lifestyle by posting your updates on social media regarding the before and after photos of having implemented the One Life, One List Lifestyle and the One Life, One list systems enclosed in this book.

Follow me on social media to let me know how you implemented the One Life, One List:

Follow me on Linkedin: Christian Moser

Follow me on Facebook: Christian Moser

Follow me on Instagram: @ChristianMoser

If you'd like some help implementing your highest productivity month ever, download my templates for organising your life here:

www.onelifeonelist.com/templates

Here are some of the templates you will be able to find in the link above:

1. Main Template
2. Weekly Planner
3. Recurring Tasks Template
4. Income Tracker Template
5. Accountability Template to manage your requests, promises and conversations
6. Shopping Template
7. My Day Template
8. Journal Template
9. Wisdom Template
10. Emergency Passport
11. Security Template

What We Have Planned For The Future

The One Life, One List app to accompany this book and this system is currently being created. We are planning to create a system that will impact 100 million people to achieve more of what they want and collaborate faster and easier on their goals through template sharing, a community that shares the values and the lifestyle of One Life, One List.

Summary

One Life, One List is the Ultimate Organisation Tool to help you gain financial, personal, choice and time freedom. Its simplicity makes it affordable for anyone who wants more out of life.

Become part of the One Life, One List freedom lifestyle community of online entrepreneurs so you, too, can work happier with ease!

Here are the principles at the core of the One Life, One List lifestyle philosophy for your review:

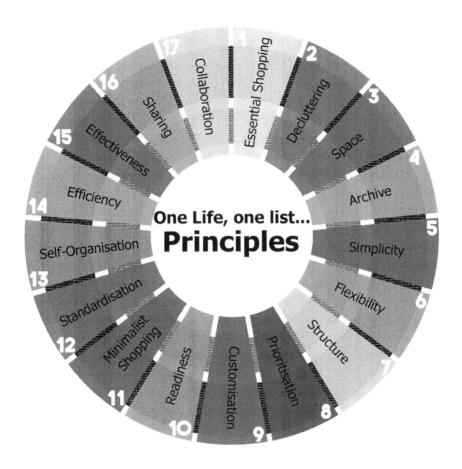

1. **Essential Shopping**
2. **Decluttering**
3. **Space**
4. **Archive**
5. **Simplicity**
6. **Flexibility**

7. **Structure**

8. **Prioritisation**

9. **Customisation**

10. **Readiness**

11. **Minimalist Shopping**

12. **Standardisation**

13. **Self-Organisation**

14. **Efficiency**

15. **Effectiveness**

16. **Sharing**

17. **Collaboration**

These are the systems at the core of the One Life, One List System:

1. **Luxury Minimalism System**

2. **Wardrobe System**

3. **Hotel System**

4. **Backpack System**

5. **Network System**

6. **Travel System**

7. **Emergency System**

8. **Security System**

9. **Office System**

10. **Stack System**

11. **Notation System**

12. **Income Tracker System**

13. **Excellent Habits System**

14. **Accountability System**

15. **Self-Reflection System**

16. **Well-Being System**

17. **Wisdom System**

18. **Relationship Management System**

19. **Balance System**

20. **Community System**

About The Author

Christian Moser is the founder of the One Life, One List philosophy of life based on the One Life, One List system for simplifying your life and your business. He is a business automation coach for creative entrepreneurs who want to create a freedom lifestyle business where they can have the freedom of choice, time and location to live their dream life.

He was awarded Freelancer Of the Year in 2011 by *IT Freelancer Magazine*. He can help you automate and systemise your business so you can double your productivity, save time and do more of what you love.

Over the last thirty-five years, Christian has empowered hundreds of small and big reputable businesses such as Bosch, Siemens, AXA, Provinzial, AIG, German Telekom, T-Mobile, Hugo Boss, Braun, John Deere, AEG, TRW, Generali, BASF, on a national and international level to create efficient ways of working and enhance their productivity by creating user-friendly efficient and effective apps, software and managing IT projects for their companies, by helping them master simple IT strategies for backing up their work, for structuring their way of working in an efficient way and by transforming the way they do business.

In his position as a developer, analyst, architect and project manager, Christian's unique outlook on IT project management involves a mix of compassionately and attentively listening to the problems the businesses face and creating user-friendly, creative IT solutions for the issues the companies have.

Christian creates the right software or apps by adapting to their needs and finally teaching them how to use them. He has a unique ability to leverage his communication skills so as to be able to understand the concerns and issues of people at every level of the organisation and knows how to touch, move and inspire the stakeholders in the business so as to reach a common objective.

Christian has created many apps in the hundreds of projects he has worked on over the years, among which the most successful is Quarta Quality Management System and Calvin Gage Management And Calibration System, which was running in thousands of companies worldwide and still does, in a newer version now developed by others.

If you have an online e-commerce business, Christian can give you IT coaching so that you can always deliver based on the promises you made to your clients. When you grow your business exponentially, you may encounter issues such as your website being down because of people intensively ordering your products online. Christian can teach you how to be prepared for all this by providing front-end and back-end IT solutions.

The author of this book has coached people all over the world, not only in using software but in applying effective and efficient processes in their companies and teams in order to optimise workflow, save time and increase productivity.

Christian has gained a high understanding of technology and the mechanisms and algorithms in our digital cloud-based future world.

He uses project management methods of Waterfall, Prince2 and agile methods based on the Scrum framework.

The founder of the One Life, One List is currently leveraging his creativity, love of music, arts and literature in his business by empowering creative entrepreneurs to have the

IT and business infrastructure to bring their ideas into the world.

Christian Moser has access to a worldwide network of successful expats, virtual entrepreneurs and inspirational coaches ready to support you achieve your goals and provide solutions for anything you may need from business automation, well-being, mindfulness, transformational coaching, public speaking, retreats in beautiful locations. These coaches will soon become part of the One Life, One List community, where freedom lifestyle gets created.

Christian deeply cares about people in need, so he actively participates in and speaks at workshops at the local Chamber of Commerce on the topic of refugees. Christian is planning to become a spokesperson for HIV awareness and for integrating refugees into the workplace.

He is an active member of the German Indonesian Society in Cologne and of the ICIS User Group of insurance companies, where he delivers keynote speeches yearly.

<u>Recommended Programmes & Seminars</u>

Create Your Own

Freedom Lifestyle Business

I have prepared a special

Freedom Lifestyle Business Masterclass

for you so that you can start practicing the <u>automation</u>, <u>systemisation</u> and <u>time freedom techniques</u> I spoke about in the book.

Discover:

- how to organise yourself with the One Life,One List system.
- ways to create your first One Life, One List
- impactful ways to dramatically change your life in 90 minutes.

Watch the **FREE** masterclass here:

<u>www.onelifeonelist.com/masterclass</u>

One Life, One List – <u>Online Course</u>

The Ultimate Organisation System

To Create A Freedom Lifestyle.

Get Access To The

www.onelifeonelist.com/onlinecourse

Here is what you will discover:

- The latest strategies for you to organise every part of your life and business with the One Life, One List system.
- The Ultimate Online Programme for creative entrepreneurs.
- Master Your Time And Productivity.
- Maximise Workflow Processes And Systems.
- Master Your Life.
- Turn A Struggling Business Into A Highly Productive One.
- Automate Your Business.

One Life, One List – <u>2-Day Intensive Workshop</u>

The Ultimate Organisation System To Create A Freedom Lifestyle.

Want To Double Your Productivity And Save Time And Money?

A 2-day intensive workshop programme suitable for corporate training, employees, CEOs, entrepreneurs, and ordinary people wanting to double their productivity and clear their workload faster, more efficiently and more effectively. This could lead to huge savings, an increase in profitability, a heightened motivation and engagement with the workload at hand, and increased happiness, too, thanks to simplification of tasks and easier task tracking. It can reduce hassle, headaches, work-related stress and it can prevent millions in lost money because of lost productivity.

This programme will help you get the latest cutting-edge techniques to automate, systemise, and leverage your time, money and experience so you can excel in your business and take your business to the next level.

Book your ticket here: www.onelifeonelist.com/workshop

If you have a group of people willing to do the 2-day seminar in your country, send **me** a proposal so I can consider flying there to deliver the workshop for your company or a group of entrepreneurs.

One Life, One List –

2-Day Multi-Speaker Event

The Ultimate Organisation System To Create A Freedom Lifestyle

A 2-day multi-speaker programme with world class experts, celebrities and entrepreneurs who have succeeded in their business.

This programme will help you get the latest cutting-edge techniques to automate, systemise, and leverage your time, money and experience so you can excel in your business and take your business to the next level. Topics that may get covered are exponential growth, simplification of your company's workflow and leveraging your employees' experience, time and money in order to enhance your bottom line.

Book your ticket here: www.onelifeonelist.com/seminar
If you have a group of people willing to do the 2-day seminar in your country, send me a proposal so I can consider flying there alongside other celebrities, world-class experts and successful entrepreneurs in my network.

Speaking Engagements

You can book me for keynote speaking engagements, for content speaking or for presentations regarding One Life, One List at hello@onelifeonelist.com

You can also let me know the need for specific other keynote speakers you need, because I am able to put you in touch with thousands of experts in their field for particular trendy topics like automation, motivation, exponential growth, speaking confidently, empowerment.

Home Learning Products

You can visit: www.onelifeonelist.com for other books or products related to automating and systemising your business and helping you create a higher profit and lower waste business.

Strategic Alliances

If you have a business proposal or joint venture idea to collaborate with me, please email me at hello@onelifeonelist.com

Templates:

Download my templates for organising your life here: www.onelifeonelist.com/templates

Social Media:

I would highly appreciate a review on Amazon.

Follow me on social media and let me know which techniques from this book have worked for your business. Register on my website if you would like to be kept updated about upcoming workshops, seminars and the upcoming community of freedom lifestyle entrepreneurs of One Life, One List.

Subscribe to One Life, One List Podcast

Follow me on LinkedIn: Christian Moser

Follow me on Facebook: Christian Moser

Follow me on Instagram: @thechristianmoser

Website: www.thechristianmoser.com

www.onelifeonelist.com

Other Books Recommended By Brand For Speakers Programme:

Speakers Are Leaders:
Empower Yourself To Start Your Speaking Career

Lily Patrascu & Harry Sardinas

Peak Performance Sales:
Turbocharge Your Sales Without Being Pushy

Lily Patrascu

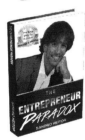

Born To Stand Out, Not To Fit In:
Empower Yourself To Live An Extraordinary Life

Teuta Avdyli

Reinvent Yourself:
Discover The Brilliance Within & Create Infinite Possibilities

Adaobi Onyekweli

The Entrepreneur Paradox:
The Easy Way To Achieve Balance & Wealth

Sandro Heitor

Dare To Be Imperfect:
Stop Doubting Yourself And Go After What Your Want

Jimmy Asuni

Whatever It Takes:
5 Minutes A Day To Motivate Yourself & Achieve Your Goals

Victor Pabon